Divine Strategies for Increase

By Steve Backlund

Acknowledgements
Editing: Leslie Taylor, Heidi O'Brien
Front and Back Cover Design: Wendy Backlund, Linda Lee

Copyright 2010 by Steve Backlund

All rights reserved. This book is protected by the copyright laws of the United States of America. This book may not be copied or reprinted for commercial gain or profit. The use of short quotations or occasional page copying for personal or group study is permitted and encouraged. Unless otherwise identified, Scripture quotations are from the New King James Version. Copyright 1982 by Thomas Nelson, Inc. Used by permission. All rights reserved. All emphasis within Scripture (besides italics) is the author's own. Please note that the author's publishing style capitalizes certain pronouns in Scripture that refer to the Father, Son and Holy Spirit, and may differ from other publisher's styles.

ISBN: 978-0-578-06524-3

Table of Contents

PART ONE – TRUTHS ABOUT SPIRITUAL LAWS

Title	Page
We Are Born for Increase	11
Sharon Stone's Karma Statement About China	12
2 Chronicles 7:14: Path to National Well-Being	13
Solomon's Prosperity Releasing Request	14
Second Generation Christians Are the Key	15
A Holistic Approach to Spiritual Laws	16
A Message for Elected Officials	17
God's Judgments or Consequences?	18
Speaking the Law	19
There Are No Sovereign Curses Put on People	20
Walking Off a Two Story Spiritual Roof	21
Are We Unenlightened Simpletons?	22
Must I Experience Curses Caused by Others?	23
What Happened at Obed-Edom's House?	24
Jesus Became a Curse for Us	25
Spiritual Laws Transcend Natural Laws	26
Prophetic Acts Impact Future Experience	27
Empowering Grace Released or Blocked	28
Delighting in the Law or Obeying Rules	29
Doesn't the Law Only Cause More Sin?	30
The Spiritual Force of Revival	31
Overcoming the Debt Mentality	32
It is Impossible for Nothing to Happen	33
Transitioning Into the Season of Increase	34
Mad Spiritual Scientists Experimenting	35

Table of Contents (Continued)

PART TWO – A SAMPLING OF SPIRITUAL LAWS

Title	Page
The Law of Giving and Generosity	39
The Law of Kingdom Priorities	40
The Law of Honesty and Integrity	41
The Law of Effort and Diligence	42
The Law of Humility	43
The Law of Association	44
The Law of Faithfulness in Small Things	45
The Law of Spiritual Inheritance	46
The Law of Caring for the Poor	47
The Law of Words	48
The Law of Forgiveness	49
The Law of Sexual Purity	50
The Law of Blessing Israel	51
The Law of Covenants	52
The Law of Sabbath Rest	53
The Law of Personal Identity	54
The Law of Unity and Agreement	55
The Law of Tithing	56
The Law of the Spirit of Life in Christ Jesus	57
The Law of Hearing	58
Other Laws	59

INTRODUCTION

In the Parable of the Talents (see Matthew 25:14-30), there is an assumption that those who were given talents would find a way to INCREASE them. They were not to adopt a passive approach of waiting for God (in His sovereignty) to do something, but they were to find righteous ways to increase what they had. These ways are God's spiritual laws.

Laws can be seen either as rules to obey or as principles to unlock the unlimited resources of the spirit realm. Solomon tapped into the latter perspective in an incredible way. His wisdom ushered in a level of national well-being that was astounding. He shares much of this revelation in the book of Proverbs.

Solomon built upon his father David's foundation of abandoned love for God to create an environment of great prosperity, safety, ingenuity and influence. Solomon pulled in abundant blessings from the spirit realm and significantly increased the "talents" he was given. Like Solomon, we too must find the means to increase what we have. We are called to bring to the nations the blessings of salvation, healing, safety, provision, shelter, soul restoration and more. To do this, we must get a heavenly strategy to multiply our talents so that we can have the abundance needed to bring transformation. Divine Strategies for Increase is written to help you INCREASE your resources so that you might be a part of changing the world like never before. Enjoy the book and get ready for MORE!

You can use this book in the following ways:
- Read it straight through to get saturated with its truth.
- Read it as a daily devotional alone or with family members.
- Participate in a group study using the book.

Part One

Truths About Spiritual Laws

Truths About Spiritual Laws #1
We Are Born for Increase

"I . . . hid your talent in the ground" (Matthew 25:25)

The Parable of the Talents in Matthew 25:14-30 teaches two powerful lessons. The first is that we have been given varying amounts of "talents." Secondly, God believes that we will find legitimate ways to increase our talents.

A talent is literally an amount of money. We know that scripture teaches us that proper attitudes and habits toward money are a training ground for having true spiritual riches released to us (see Luke 16:11), but the lessons of this parable go far beyond just finances.

Each of us has been given a certain set of beginning circumstances in life that could be considered our talents. These "talents" will be more for some people and less for others. Whatever our situation, one thing is clear: We are called to increase what we have. And we know that God never commands us to do something without providing the way to perform it.

The two faithful servants in the Parable of the Talents found ways to increase what they had. We too are to find the means to increase our abilities, our positive influence and numerous other aspects of life. One of the main ways we do this is by accessing the spiritual laws that God has established. As we do, we will see the increase. We will not be like the unfaithful one in this parable who hid his talent out of fear and a faulty concept of God, but we'll harness these spiritual laws to work for us just as mankind has harnessed natural laws like gravity.

We are created with a DNA for growth and increase. Indeed, the kingdom only moves forward through those who increase their talents. The Great Commission of Matthew 28:18-20 can only accelerate if there are those who are enlarging who they are, and who are obtaining more power, love, divine strategies, success in relationships, finances, physical health, protection and anointing. Because of this reality, we have confidence that we can and will increase.

We must believe we are to **PROSPER** (increase our talents) to have God's will done through us. Some reject the prosperity message because of doctrinal imbalances, selfishness and other abuses that have come from some of its most vocal proponents. We cannot overreact to this error and miss the vital necessity of increasing what we have. We may not become rich in the eyes of others, but we must believe for and pursue greater resources so that we will more and more become a source of salvation and miracles to others.

Truths About Spiritual Laws #2
Sharon Stone's Karma Statement About China
"It is because . . . Saul . . . killed the Gibeonites" (2 Samuel 21:1)

Sharon Stone raised eyebrows and created anger in May of 2008 when she wondered aloud if a recent devastating earthquake in China was "karma" for China's mistreatment of the Tibetan people. She was strongly criticized for being insensitive to the plight of the suffering Chinese—and for believing there was a connection between the actions of the government and "natural events" like earthquakes. She later apologized and recanted her statements.

I don't know if there was any connection between Tibet and the earthquake, but moral choices do influence future blessing or the lack thereof. This is confirmed by the following story in the Old Testament:

King David had a lingering difficulty that is described in 2 Samuel 21. There was a famine over Israel that had lasted three years. After this time (and presumably praying for relief), he inquired of the Lord. "And the LORD answered, '*It is* because of Saul and *his* bloodthirsty house, because he killed the Gibeonites'" (2 Samuel 21:1). The Israelites had sworn to protect these people, but Saul had broken this promise. This caused the famine, and it wouldn't end until this curse in the spirit realm was acknowledged, renounced and corrected.

This is an incredibly enlightening story for us. Saul, David's predecessor, violated a covenant, and it produced a famine decades later. This national crisis was not brought about by climatic change or other reasons. It was the result of a negative seed that was planted into the spiritual atmosphere by the carelessness of the nation's government.

Ending this famine required someone who believed in the reality of spiritual laws. Secular advisors could not help in identifying its root cause. David, fortunately, was a man with a supernatural world-view, and he took the necessary spiritual steps to reverse this curse of a famine (and the whole nation benefited as a result).

Sharon Stone got one thing right. Moral choices, such as how we treat people, will affect the level of protection a nation has from disasters like earthquakes or famines. Those of us who answer God's call to **PROSPER** have the privilege of reversing curses in our lives, families, churches, regions and nation. Those who come after us will be glad that we did!

Truths About Spiritual Laws #3
2 Chronicles 7:14: Path to National Well-Being

"If My people will . . . pray . . . then I will heal their land" (2 Chronicles 7:14)

Let me ask you a question. Who "controls" climatic weather patterns, the economy, and the physical health of a nation? One well-known Bible verse shows us the answer. "If **My people** who are called by My name will humble themselves and pray and seek My face and turn from their wicked ways, **then I** will hear from heaven, forgive their sin, and **heal their land**" (2 Chronicles 7:14).

God has empowered His people to remedy (heal) the ills of nations. In 2 Chronicles 7:13-14, we see three areas of life that we are commissioned to heal. God said, "When I shut up heaven and there is no rain (**climate and weather problems**), or command the locusts to devour the land (**economic difficulties**) or send pestilence (**plagues and health problems**)." After He listed these forms of national suffering, He said, "If My people . . . then I will heal their land."

It's enlightening to understand that we (God's people) are in more control than we might think concerning these three foundational areas of life: climate, economy, and health. We are not "victims" of non-believers, but the world is a victim to us if we are not walking in true humility and authority. We are the head, not the tail. We are above and not beneath. (See Deuteronomy 28:13.) Even if non-believers create a mess through ongoing disobedience of spiritual laws; God's people can reverse this and bring national healing and PROSPERITY through humility, prayer, seeking His face and by turning to delighting in His laws.

The world cannot stop the church. We have more influence than we probably know. Scripture says that "One can put a thousand to flight; two, ten thousand" (Deuteronomy 32:30). As we walk in the revelation of who God says we are, things will change. This does not mean we never speak about the sins of our nation, but our primary focus must be to instill biblical identity in the believers we influence. As we do so, we will be doing the greatest thing we can in affecting the roots of our country's well-being and quality of life. This is a true act of love that those who come after us will be eternally thankful for.

Note: It is important to know that these negative circumstances are "sent by God" only in the sense that He has set up spiritual laws that if violated will cause the weakening of spiritual protection in the land. He does not choose this pain to happen, but it is caused by repetitive violations of spiritual laws.

Truths About Spiritual Laws #4
Solomon's Prosperity Releasing Request

"Ask! What shall I give you?" (2 Chronicles 1:7)

If God told you He would give you whatever you asked for, what would you ask for? Well, Solomon, King David's son and successor, had this happen to him. Here's the story. "On that night God appeared to Solomon, and said to him, '**Ask! What shall I give you?**' And Solomon said to God: 'You have shown great mercy to David my father, and have made me king in his place. Now, O LORD God, **let Your promise** to David my father **be established**, for You have made me king over a people like the dust of the earth in multitude. **Now give me wisdom and knowledge**, that I may go out and come in before this people; for who can judge this great people of Yours?'" (2 Chronicles 1:7-10).

When Solomon asked for wisdom and knowledge, God was moved and impressed. "Then God said to Solomon: 'Because this was in your heart, and you have not asked for riches or wealth or honor or the life of your enemies, nor have you asked long life—but have asked wisdom . . . wisdom and knowledge *are* granted to you; **and I will give you riches and wealth and honor**, such as none of the kings have had who *were* before you, nor shall any after you have the like'" (2 Chronicles 1:11-12). An incredible blessing of the Lord would be released because of the greatness of his request.

King Solomon concluded that David's zeal alone was not enough to see revival sustained. He honored his father but also realized that David's passions and relational weaknesses created a breakdown in protection and blessing over his family. The pain of this may have caused the new king to swing the pendulum too far in the direction of principles (spiritual laws) and away from spiritual intimacy; but God still was delighted by Solomon's discernment about what Israel needed in its next season. God will feel the same regarding many of us who are also living in a time where a supernatural revelation of wisdom is needed.

What was the result of Solomon's revelation of how spiritual laws operate? First, the book of Proverbs emerged. It is the life-giving manual on spiritual laws. Secondly, it created unprecedented national prosperity for Israel. 2 Chronicles 9 reveals the greatness of wealth, happiness, wisdom, fame and influence that resulted from a leader who committed himself to have revelation about the laws of the Spirit. Yes, we are aware that Solomon ended poorly and left a mess behind him, but that does not negate our need to find the heart of Solomon's PROSPERITY-releasing request. Accelerated kingdom advancement depends on it.

Truths About Spiritual Laws #5
Second Generation Christians Are the Key
"Keep your spiritual fervor" (Romans 12:11)

There is a similarity seen in Scripture about the traits of first, second and third generational believers. This instructive pattern is supported by what is regularly seen in the lives and ministries of Christians. Solomon and his generational relationships illustrate this powerfully.

First generation believers and ministries are those who have had a transforming spiritual experience. Their testimony is, "Once I was blind and now I see." They have a revelation that they have been forgiven much, so they love much. They are marked by passion, sacrifice, evangelism, spiritual hunger, love for the supernatural, risk taking and emotional intimacy with God. They value the apostolic and prophetic ministries because they create an even greater "open heaven" of spiritual life. However, first generation believers often struggle with impulsiveness, with not planning for the future, and with relationships (family and otherwise).

The second generation represents the sons and daughters (both physically and spiritually) of those ignited by spiritual fire. They have been raised up in the presence of God that was created by the sacrifice and warfare of the first generation. They didn't need to fight for what they have. These sons and daughters tend to value principles more than presence; teachers, pastors and administrators more than apostles and prophets; predictability over spontaneity; programs over intimacy; and building structure over pursuing fresh encounters with God. Yes, the second generation will need to make adjustments to correct negative tendencies of their predecessors, but many do not do this successfully because they have drifted away from a passionate love for God and His presence.

The first generation is likely to have a full heart for God. The second generation is prone to be half-hearted and have a lesser desire to seek Him as their fathers did. This non-passionate attitude and their being prone to excessively focus on principles and building things creates a powerless environment for the **third generation** to live in (with backsliding and godlessness the result).

You can find many of these generational tendencies in Solomon's family line of David (first generation), Solomon (second) and Rehoboam (third). It is also seen in Abraham, Isaac and Jacob.

So what is the answer? The first generation must do as David did in empowering their children to greatness, but the second generation and succeeding generations must keep seeking God's face, not just His hand or words of wisdom. Then PROPSERITY will be maintained and increased.

Truths About Spiritual Laws #6
A Holistic Approach to Spiritual Laws

"Write **them** on the tablet of your heart" (Proverbs 3:3)

There is a growing emphasis in the holistic treatment of physical ailments. This medical approach considers all factors that may be contributing to poor health. For instance, instead of only treating the symptoms of a headache with pain medicine, there will be a thorough exploration of how other factors may contribute to the problem (i.e. nutrition, sleep patterns, exercise, coping with stress, etc.). The holistic method in medicine helps in getting to the root of sickness, and it greatly improves the overall well-being and health of the individual.

A holistic approach to spiritual laws is also needed for personal success, to advance the kingdom and to leave a blessing to our descendents. We must consider the overall spectrum of the laws of the Spirit—whether to get out of a difficulty or to pursue a dream to increase our talents. We cannot just give our attention to that which seems directly related to our crisis or dream. We can be strong in one law, but not reap the benefits because of a major violation of another. For instance, a person can give greatly in finances (the law of generosity); but because of unworthiness (the law of identity), future blessing is restricted. It's like having the heater on with the door open (the gains are lost).

When we follow God's truth in an area and conclude "It's not working;" it is advisable to take a holistic approach concerning our situation. For instance, some pray well, but their word curses after prayer undoes things. Others receive great wisdom about healthy relationships, but a spirit of fear or bitterness blocks powerful heart connections from occurring. It is easy to fall into the trap of focusing on only one law in our zeal to overcome and grow, but a holistic perspective gets more results.

Let's conclude this teaching by considering what a holistic approach to financial blessing would look like. Again, it is easy to emphasize just one truth such as giving or tithing as the key to breakthrough. Certainly, we don't discount the many biblical promises of increased finances through faithful giving. However, many preachers only emphasize generosity, and consequently there are multitudes of disillusioned people who have not reaped what they expected. A holistic view would not only discuss giving; but also would concentrate on other spiritual laws such as faith, kingdom priorities, words, diligence, integrity, creativity, love, unity and gratefulness. We don't need to be perfect to be blessed, but the wise believer will take a holistic approach to see if there are blatant violations of spiritual laws that limit the flow of success and PROSPERITY.

Truths About Spiritual Laws #7
A Message for Elected Officials
"Righteousness exalts a nation" (Proverbs 14:34)

"It's about the economy, stupid" is a phrase that supposedly helps politicians have proper priorities. Many political leaders have heard an earful of complaints when they have supposedly "dropped the ball" concerning the financial security of those they lead. The message implies that a prosperous nation results from an emphasis on such things as taxes or laws that affect businessess. Indeed, we don't discount the importance of having laws that empower people, but a nation's long-term blessing comes from good moral choices (not from astute political decisions or charismatic leaders).

I am an American citizen. I believe that my country has had enduring abundance and protection because of honoring God's laws. The USA has sown positive seeds into the spirit realm through its generosity (see 2 Corinthians 9:6), by sending a multitude of missionaries into the nations (see Matthew 6:33), by honoring its people (see Proverbs 29:14), by supporting Israel (see Genesis 12:3), and in other ways as well. Has America followed all of God's laws, and is everything about America wonderful? Obviously no, but it is an example of what can happen if a nation's leaders think long-term and intentionally sow righteousness. America's greatness has not been by happenstance. It resulted from a people who knew what was really important.

The biblical account of Israel reinforces what I am teaching. Righteousness does exalt a nation (see Proverbs 14:34). I suggest you read Judges, I & II Kings and I & II Chronicles to see this truth demonstrated. The blessing on the land and its people was directly related to whether they had a good leader who honored God and His ways.

These truths are for every nation and city. The story about the depraved city of Nineveh in the book of Jonah reveals that spiritual protection can be quickly re-established when a leader and his people respond to the prophetic warning that disaster is coming. The King of Nineveh realized what every political leader must know. Morality is the key to a nation with a happy people.

Note: Heart change is better than legislating morality. It is instructional to see the progression of the positive spiritual steps in 2 Chronicles 7:14: 1) humility, 2) prayer, 3) seek His face, and 4) turn from wicked ways. The turning from harmful moral choices (#4) will be increasingly likely if we get #'s 1-3 right. Also, morality is more than sexuality (which is vital); it is also about integrity, protecting the weak, keeping covenants, forgiving, making restitution and having a saving faith in Jesus.

Truths About Spiritual Laws #8
God's Judgments or Consequences?

"Whatever a man sows, that he will also reap" (Galatians 6:7)

The Bible speaks a great deal about justice and judgment. The Old Testament, especially, is full of verses and stories that illustrate the blessing of the righteous and the judgment of the unrighteous. What should we conclude about this? Is this an angry God punishing people and nations with judgment when they displease Him? Does He use fear of punishment as the primary motivating force to get us to behave? Is our Heavenly Father like an abusive parent with anger issues that may erupt at any time in destruction and death?

Before we consider these questions, it is important to remember that justice does demand judgment of sin. In the Old Testament, God's wrath was directed at people and nations who were disobedient. However, everything changed when He placed all of His wrath on Jesus at the cross. "But He *was* wounded for our transgressions, *He was* bruised for our iniquities; the chastisement for our peace *was* upon Him, and by His stripes we are healed" (Isaiah 53:5). Jesus took our judgment and offers us His abundant life in exchange. We receive this through faith in Him.

Even though God poured out His wrath on Jesus, there are still apparent judgments on people and nations today. Why? Space does not allow a thorough discussion of this, but the question for me boils down to this: Should these events be called judgments (punishment) or consequences? I have concluded we are to primarily see them as consequences. It is similar to the dynamics that exist when a parent disciplines a child. In healthy parenting, it is the actions and choices of the child that create the discomfort and restriction of freedom, not the anger of the parent.

Just as a child reaps what he sows, so can we today. Whenever there is a persistent violation of spiritual laws, the protection and blessing over a person, family line, region or nation begins to lift. This lessening of spiritual protection allows increased disasters, poverty and control by others. This has been true throughout history (before Moses, during the Old Covenant and now in the New Covenant). Yes, the spiritual laws of inheritance, faith and blessing can supersede the law of sowing and reaping, but we would be foolish to not believe that our relationship to the laws of the spirit plays a significant role in the amount of blessing and protection that is experienced. The people of Nineveh (see Jonah 3:1-10) understood this. They believed the prophet and reversed the curse of destruction through humility, prayer, seeking God and renouncing godless choices. Just as they did, so can we! Praise the Lord.

Truths About Spiritual Laws #9
Speaking the Law

"This book of the law shall not depart from your mouth" (Joshua 1:8)

Joshua was promoted to replace Moses because of three compelling reasons: 1) **He was a man who knew God intimately.** "So the LORD spoke to Moses face to face, as a man speaks to his friend. And he would return to the camp, but his servant Joshua the son of Nun, a young man, did not depart from the tabernacle" (Exodus 33:11). 2) **He saw breakthrough and victory where others saw defeat and death.** "But Joshua . . . and Caleb . . . tore their clothes, and . . . spoke . . . saying: 'Do not . . . fear the people of the land, for they *are* our bread; their protection has departed from them, and the LORD *is* with us. Do not fear them.'" 3) **Joshua also had supernatural wisdom received through spiritual inheritance and impartation.** "Now Joshua the son of Nun was full of the spirit of wisdom, for Moses had laid his hands on him" (Deuteronomy 34:9).

Joshua represents a new breed of leader who is full of intimacy, abounding hope, supernatural wisdom and is accustomed to signs and wonders. Joshua was uniquely positioned and was seemingly ready to lead God's people into their destiny. However, in the first chapter of Joshua, we read that there was some final polishing of Joshua's leadership gift that was needed. He was admonished to stir up white-hot courage in his life and was told, "This Book of the Law shall not depart from your mouth, but you shall meditate in it day and night, that you may observe to do according to all that is written in it. For then you will make your way prosperous, and then you will have good success" (Joshua 1:8).

Wow, wow, wow! Joshua was told that the final step to experiencing triumph and abundance would be started by continually speaking about the Book of the Law. He was told to not let it depart from his *mouth*—as opposed to his mind or heart. He was to speak continually about the wonders of God and His spiritual laws. (I am sure he did not focus on the "Thou shalt nots" but went up to the headwaters of God's nature and promises that each law represented!) This truth of speaking God's laws is reinforced by understanding that one of the meanings of "meditate" in verse eight is "to talk to yourself."

I have written extensively in You're Crazy If You DON'T Talk to Yourself about regularly needing to hear truth to upgrade our beliefs so we can walk in greater things in the days ahead. "So then faith *comes* by hearing, and hearing by the word of God" (Romans 10:17). We cannot just study God's laws; we must speak them. Let's go for it and speak things like: "Honor releases life. God honors me. I honor others. I release life by honor." We won't be sorry we did.

Truths About Spiritual Laws #10
There Are No Sovereign Curses Put on People

"A curse without cause shall not alight" (Proverbs 26:2)

A curse is a spiritual force that works against the success, protection, health and relationships of a person or group of people. It creates an environment where much effort yields little reward. Deuteronomy 28 lists many symptoms of being under a curse. These include unfruitfulness, sickness, poverty and failure. On the contrary, blessing creates success far beyond what is deserved. (Think about what happened to Obed Edom's house in 2 Samuel 6:10-12.) We will study the force of blessing later.

"A curse without cause shall not alight" (Proverbs 26:2). In other words, there is always a root reason for the blessing's decrease and the curse's corresponding increase. Curses do not result from some random happening of chance, nor is it an act of God's sovereignty that predestinated some for abundant life and others for hardship. There is a cause to every curse.

This awareness can be both discouraging and encouraging. It can discourage us because we realize that our choices and beliefs have contributed to our negative circumstances. However, it encourages us as we understand that we can reverse the curse in us and around us.

Haggai 1:6-7,9 dramatically illustrates the effects of a curse. "You have sown much, and bring in little; you eat, but do not have enough; you drink, but you are not filled with drink; you clothe yourselves, but no one is warm; And he who earns wages, earns wages *to put* into a bag with holes. Thus says the LORD of hosts: 'Consider your ways . . . *You* looked for much, but indeed *it came to* little; and when you brought it home, I blew it away. Why?' says the LORD of hosts. 'Because of My house that *is in* ruins, while every one of you runs to his own house. Therefore the heavens above you withhold the dew, and the earth withholds its fruit. For I called for a drought on the land and the mountains, on the grain and the new wine and the oil, on whatever the ground brings forth, on men and livestock, and on all the labor of *your* hands.'" God described what happened to them (being unfruitful, difficulty, frustration, etc.). Then He gives the cause for this curse: "Because of my house that is in ruins." They violated the law of kingdom priority (see Matthew 6:33).

In Haggai, the people didn't think they were victims of rotten luck, but they believed the prophetic word that revealed the curse had a cause that they could remedy (which they did). They were not discouraged or hopeless when they heard this, but empowered. We can be, too!

Truths About Spiritual Laws #11
Walking Off a Two Story Spiritual Roof

"Whoever listens to me will dwell safely" (Proverbs 1:33)

I wrote the following in Igniting Faith in 40 Days:

Can you imagine someone walking off a two-story roof, breaking his leg and then blaming God for what happened? That would be ridiculous. Well, that is in essence what many do by ignoring the laws of the Spirit.

Law is "a scientific fact or phenomenon that is invariable under given conditions" (Encarta World English Dictionary). The law of gravity is an example of this. It needs to be understood and allowed to control everyday decisions or there could be serious consequences!

It is also foolish to not live by spiritual laws—which are just as real and also must be grasped and applied. Scripture speaks of these laws or principles that govern the spiritual dimension—which ultimately control the natural dimension that we live in. It is important that we understand that there are truths to be esteemed for safe and successful living (whether it is the law of honor, agreement, sexual purity, sowing and reaping, tithing, faith or speaking life). Only a fool would think that our choices, thoughts and words have no consequences.

So, are you walking off a two-story roof in the spirit realm and thinking you can defy the laws of the Spirit? It won't work. You'll get hurt. Cry out now for the heavenly wisdom to know what is real and true. You won't be sorry. You'll be blessed.

These words draw us further into the truth that there are obvious long-term consequences (positive and negative) resulting from our relationship with spiritual laws. As we close today's teaching, consider what we would find if we took someone who honored God's laws for 50 years and someone who did not – and then stood them side by side. What do you think we would discover? In most cases we would find:

Honoring Laws	**Blatant Disobeying of Laws**
Quality relationships	Relationship breakdown
Loving and hopeful	Fearful and cynical
Growing protection	Protection weakening
Face soft & young looking	Face hardened & aged

Truths About Spiritual Laws #12
Are We Unenlightened Simpletons?

"The fool has said in his heart, '*There is* no God.'" (Psalm 14:1)

The book of Jonah is filled with people who had a "spiritual laws worldview." The end portion of chapter one is an example of this. The sailors believed that a severe storm was caused by the actions of someone on the ship. They pressed into this belief and discovered Jonah was the reason for the tumult. Jonah said that the storm would cease if they threw him overboard. "Nevertheless the men rowed hard to return to land, but they could not, for the sea continued to grow more tempestuous against them. Therefore they cried out to the LORD and said, 'We pray, O LORD, please do not let us perish for this man's life, and do not charge us with innocent blood; for You, O LORD, have done as it pleased You.' So they picked up Jonah and threw him into the sea, and the sea ceased from its raging. Then the men feared the LORD exceedingly, and offered a sacrifice to the LORD and took vows" (Jonah 1:13-16).

Here are more examples in Jonah about spiritual laws:

- Jonah's repentance and cries to God caused the fish to vomit him out of bondage and into freedom (Jonah 2:10).
- Jonah proclaimed that Nineveh's spiritual protection was going to be gone in 40 days (Jonah 3:4). This future influx of curses was caused by their "evil ways and violence" (3:8).
- Nineveh's positive response cancelled the looming curse and reestablished protection over them (Jonah 3:10).

Many would say that the people of Jonah's time were unenlightened simpletons whose worldview needs to be rejected as only harmful, fear-producing superstition. Yes, we do recognize that there have been some extremely weird beliefs concerning spiritual laws, but we cannot reactively go to the other extreme in blindly embracing secularism as our new religion. Any mindset that rejects the **cause and effect** created by moral choices, beliefs and treatment of others would be much more dangerous in the long run. It not only influences people away from God, but it causes messes for future generations to clean up.

So, how do we help the supposedly enlightened people around us who discount spiritual realities? Logic and reasoning can be helpful, but Paul gives us the real answer. "And my speech and my preaching *were* not with persuasive words of human wisdom, but in demonstration of the Spirit and of power, that your faith should not be in the wisdom of men but in the power of God" (1 Corinthians 2:4-5). It is hard to argue with an "unenlightened simpleton" who walks in power. Praise the Lord!

Truths About Spiritual Laws #13
Must I Experience Curses Caused by Others?

"But it shall not come near you" (Psalm 91:7)

Do believers have to suffer because others violate God's laws and disrupt corporate spiritual protection? Should we expect our lives to be difficult because we are connected to someone running from God or making really poor choices (like those on the ship with Jonah)? These are important questions as we establish victorious mindsets for our lives.

In answering these questions, consider Psalm 91. "A thousand may fall at your side, and ten thousand at your right hand; **but it shall not come near you** . . . Because you have made the LORD, *who is* my refuge, *even* the Most High, your dwelling place, no evil shall befall you, **nor shall any plague come near your dwelling**" (Psalm 91:7-10). The psalmist boldly declares that he has personal protection from corporate curses. He proclaims that there is a supernatural defense available to shield the individual from disasters in his environment. He says this will be experienced by those who dwell in His secret place, who love Him, who call on Him and who know His name. (See vs. 1, 9, 14,15).

I am intrigued by the belief system of the psalmist. Even though he lived under an inferior covenant to ours (see Hebrews 8:6), he seems to say, "No matter what difficulties others face, I have a special protection with God that safeguards me from the negative things that are happening in my surroundings." Is he declaring a spiritual reality that is available to all, or is he referring to something that is only for a few select believers in unique situations?

One struggle in applying Psalm 91 is the consideration of people in the Bible who were not protected from problems around them. For example, Joshua and Caleb spent 40 years with self-inflicted wanderers, Daniel lived in restriction because of his nation's sins, and Christians in Acts were persecuted and martyred. Should we let the experience of these godly ones tone down our beliefs about personal protection? No. If we do lessen our expectations, then we are assuming that these were living at the highest level of their covenant with God. (This is not true as Jesus was the only one who did so.) Conclusions based on the experiences of others will lower our beliefs and ultimately lessen our life experience. Yes, Jesus suffered when He **chose** to be crucified, but His life was all about supernatural protection and provision (no matter what was going on around Him). He is our example, but more importantly, He created the way for us to be treated as He deserves, not as we deserve, through His death and resurrection. This includes forgiveness, health, power, abundant provision and SUPERNATURAL PROTECTION regardless of the circumstances. Praise the Lord! Let's believe to increasingly see His protection and blessing.

Truths About Spiritual Laws #14
What Happened at Obed-Edom's House?

"The Lord has blessed Obed-Edom . . . because of the ark" (2 Sam. 6:12)

One story that illustrates the power of blessing is in 2 Samuel 6. "So David would not move the ark of the LORD with him into the City of David; but David took it aside into the house of Obed-Edom the Gittite. The ark of the LORD remained in the house of Obed-Edom the Gittite three months. And the LORD blessed Obed-Edom and all his household. Now it was told King David, saying, 'The LORD has blessed the house of Obed-Edom and all that *belongs* to him, because of the ark of God.' So David went and brought up the ark of God from the house of Obed-Edom to the City of David with gladness" (2 Samuel 6:10-12).

Obed-Edom's experience was remarkable. He was a Gentile who served David (possibly as a bodyguard). He had the fortunate experience of having the Ark of the Covenant come to his house for three months. The result of this was incredible. Scripture says, "The Lord blessed Obed-Edom and his household." Wow! I wonder what the blessing looked like? What would you have seen if you were his neighbor?

A blessing is a spiritual force that causes success, protection and happiness beyond what is deserved. An understanding of blessing and curses is foundational to a study on God's spiritual laws. Even though curses are real, it is important to know that blessings are more powerful (just as light is more powerful than darkness).

Those observing Obed-Edom's blessing must have seen some astonishing things to have the report even get to the king. What do you think his neighbors saw? Let me speculate. I believe they observed most or all of these things: relational healing and joy in the family, faces glowing with God's glory, vegetation thriving, profound wisdom, deep intimacy with the Lord, confidence, peace, supernatural power, success in everything they did, unusual "luck," financial prosperity, favor, physical vitality, protection and the ability to create blessing wherever they went.

What did Obed-Edom do to receive all these kingdom benefits? He basically did nothing to receive this free gift of life (this grace). He was the benefactor of a spiritual force called blessing. His experience speaks that there are higher ways of living available to us. Indeed, our New Covenant benefits are greater than the power of the Ark. God's heart is not only that we are blessed, but, more importantly, that we become a blessing. Let's become a blessing by building our faith in the power of blessing and intentionally releasing this undeserved transforming grace wherever we go.

Truths About Spiritual Laws #15
Jesus Became a Curse for Us

"Christ has redeemed us from the curse of the law" (Galatians 3:13)

Here is some thrilling good news. "**Christ has redeemed us from the curse of the law**, having become a curse for us (for it is written, *'Cursed is everyone who hangs on a tree'*) that the blessing of Abraham might come upon the Gentiles in Christ Jesus, that we might receive the promise of the Spirit through faith" (Galatians 3:13-14). Jesus took all the curses that I deserved because of the choices made by my ancestors and me. He offers to me a great exchange. If I give Him the curses I earn because of violating His spiritual laws, then He will give us the blessing of Abraham that He merited through His sinless life of never breaking a spiritual law. We receive this gift by grace through faith. This is a tremendous aspect of the good news of our salvation!

Galatians 3:13-14 says that Jesus did not just remove our curses from us but actually became a curse for us. This has profound meaning. Jesus not only took the negative consequences of sinful choices, but He actually struck a death blow to our cursed nature itself. He became cursed so that we would not have to experience the cursed nature. Indeed, we are the righteousness of Christ and that certainly is not cursed. (See 2 Corinthians 5:21.)

To help us understand this further, consider these words that God spoke to Abram (whose name was later changed to Abraham). "I will make you a great nation; I will bless you and make your name great; and **you shall be a blessing**. I will bless those who bless you, and I will curse him who curses you; and in you all the families of the earth shall be blessed. I will make you a great nation; I will bless you and make your name great; and **you shall be a blessing**" (Genesis 12:2-2). God blessed Abraham but, incredibly, He also made him a blessing. He became like the Ark of Covenant that brought undeserved abundance and success to Obed-Edom and his household (see previous teaching).

Consider this truth: What is in us is greater than what was in the Ark of the Covenant! We are living in a superior covenant that has better promises (Hebrews 8:6). **The depth of Christ's experience in the negative (*becoming* a curse) opens the door for a correspondingly great happening in the positive (*becoming* a blessing).** Paul says "the blessing of Abraham" (Galatians 3:14) is available to us. This is activated when "we receive the promise of the Spirit through faith." Let's rejoice that the Spirit in the Ark is now in us and will bless all the families of the earth through us! Praise God!

Truths About Spiritual Laws #16
Spiritual Laws Transcend Natural Laws

"Peter . . . walked on the water to go to Jesus" (Matthew 14:29)

The Book of Acts reveals what the "normal" Christian life looks like. It is filled with supernatural events that show us what is possible in life. Here's a list of some of these happenings:

- An angel appears to people and talked with them (Acts 1:10-11)
- Sound of a heavenly wind heard and fire appears on heads (2:3)
- Life-long lame man is healed (3:8)
- Building shakes during prayer meeting (4:31)
- Peter's shadow heals people (5:15-16)
- Stephen sees into heaven, sees glory and sees Jesus (7:56)
- Philip is translated to another location instantly (8:39-40)
- Unsaved Saul sees heavenly light and has Jesus talk to him (9:3-5)
- Cornelius has a vision, and an angel speaks to him (10:3-6)
- Peter, while in a trance, hears a heavenly voice and sees a sheet full of objects coming down from heaven (10:9-13)
- Heavenly light seen, and an angel appears to help prisoner escape – and gate opens on own accord (12:7-10)
- Obstinate, disruptive sorcerer is blinded by Paul (13:8-11)
- Prayer and worship cause earthquake in prison that opens all prison doors and breaks off all shackles (16:25-28)
- Healing and delivering power is imparted into handkerchiefs and aprons by Paul (19:11-12)
- Poisonous snake bite causes no harm (28:3-6)
- All sick on island are healed (28:7-9)

The Bible is full of incidents where the spiritual laws of faith, identity, prayer, anointing and impartation caused the spirit realm to supercede the laws of nature. Nothing has changed that would stop or limit these things from happening now. Christians have unlimited potential to release supernatural happenings on earth through the power that works in them. (See Ephesians 3:20.) The laws of the natural realm are still submitted to the laws of the Spirit, and the natural must yield to the supernatural. With this great reality in our hearts, let's obey 1 Corinthians 14:1 and burn with zeal to see an invasion of the supernatural gifts of the Spirit happen through us today. Let us, like Phillip in Acts 8, become the conduit for a miraculous city-transforming power that brings great joy.

Truths About Spiritual Laws #17
Prophetic Acts Impact Future Experience

"Take the arrows . . . strike the ground" (2 Kings 13:18)

Here is a story from 2 Kings that makes you stop and wonder. "Then he (Elisha) said, 'Take the arrows;' so he took *them*. And he said to the king of Israel, 'Strike the ground'; so he struck three times, and stopped. And the man of God was angry with him, and said, 'You should have struck five or six times; then you would have struck Syria till you had destroyed *it!* But now you will strike Syria *only* three times'" (2 Kings 13:18-19). Israel's future was radically influenced by how many times the king struck the ground with an arrow! Wow! What is this all about and what meaning does this have for us today?

The king was unaware that he was involved in what is called a *prophetic act* (something intentionally done that increases God's workings in the spirit realm so positive change can come into the natural realm). He should have remembered prophetic acts like that of Moses raising his rod so that freedom and victory could be realized.

Moses used his rod prophetically in two separate instances. First, he stretched it out over the sea and the waters parted. (See Exodus 14:16, 21.) Secondly, he caused victory in a battle when the rod was lifted up. (See Exodus 17:9-13.) This second situation is mind-boggling. Whenever Moses' arms went down, the battle began to be lost. Fortunately, those around Moses (Aaron and Hur) understood prophetic acts and consequently held up Moses' arms so that victory was insured.

Unfortunately, the King of Israel was dull in his understanding of spiritual realities. He did not believe what Moses and those around him clearly believed—that what happens in the natural results from something that has already happened in the spiritual. The more we believe like Moses, the more we will proactively do prophetic acts to bring spiritual breakthrough.

So don't be surprised if you sense God telling you to do things that may seem strange. Some prophetic acts I have participated in or heard about include: driving prayer stakes into the four corners of a city or region, anointing buildings with oil, putting a stuffed Tigger on a church's stage, placing a cloth mantle on newly ordained ministers, waving flags in worship, jumping for joy during hard times, shouting and placing a Bible in the foundation of a new home. Actions like these done in faith actually do bring a positive result. Let's not be like the King of Israel who missed his defining moment, but let's purpose to respond enthusiastically to prophetic windows of opportunity that come to us.

Truths About Spiritual Laws #18
Empowering Grace Released or Blocked
"You have fallen from grace" (Galatians 5:4)

I cannot get enough of the book of Galatians. Its teachings have brought radical freedom to my life. It reveals that we must be more belief-focused than conduct-focused. If we aren't, we will slip into the folly of the Galatian Christians. "O foolish Galatians! Who has bewitched you that you should not obey the truth . . . This only I want to learn from you: Did you receive the Spirit by the works of the law, or by the hearing of faith?" (Galatians 3:1-2). Paul accuses the Galatians of being bewitched and disobedient. What was their error? Let's read more. "Are you so foolish? Having begun in the Spirit, are you now being made perfect by the flesh? . . . He who supplies the Spirit to you and works miracles among you, *does He do it* by the works of the law, or by the hearing of faith?" (Galatians 3:3-5). The Galatians were backsliding from a beliefs mindset into a works mindset. He calls this foolishness, a deception and disobedience. Hmm, let's explore why he makes such a big deal out of it.

The Old Covenant was "works driven," while the New Covenant is propelled by beliefs. The Galatians were trying to mix the two, but that cannot be successfully done. Paul reminded them that they became Christians (received the Spirit) by the hearing of faith (not by works). This hearing of faith not only gains entrance into the kingdom, but it is also the only avenue for true maturity and kingdom advancement.

The entire book of Galatians is a powerful rebuke to being more conduct-focused than belief-focused. Chapter five drives this truth home with an alarming statement about grace. "You have become estranged from Christ, you who *attempt to* be justified by law; **you have fallen from grace**" (Galatians 5:4). We normally think that falling from grace results from sinful choices, but it states here that it comes from the heresy that thinks good works move God's hand instead of faith. We must reject this deception as we seek to have the laws of the Spirit work for us and not against us. Grace is a supernatural empowerment that enables us to do God's will. Its flow is maximized when we are fully convinced that what we believe is more important than what we do. Future personal and world revival will result primarily from someone believing something, not doing something. Yes, works are important (see James 2:20), but let's be like Abraham and prioritize our beliefs to become "fully convinced that what He had promised He (is) also able to perform" (Romans 4:21). Amen!

Truths About Spiritual Laws #19
Delighting in the Law or Obeying Rules
"But his delight *is* in the law of the LORD" (Psalm 1:2)

Psalm 1 is another gold mine for those who want to unlock the potential of spiritual laws. It starts by revealing that people will be blessed (have undeserved success, protection, provision and happiness) if they:

1. **Don't walk in the counsel of the ungodly** – Blessed counsel comes through people who honor Jesus and God's laws.
2. **Don't stand in the path of sinners** – "He who walks with the wise will be wise" (Proverbs 13:20), but "Evil company corrupts good habits" (1 Corinthians 15:33). Blessing increases by aligning ourselves with people of wisdom.
3. **Don't sit in the seat of the scornful** – The attitudes of honor and humility release life so that grace and blessing will flow.

After sharing what not to do, the psalmist goes on to describe the actions of the outrageously blessed. "**But his delight *is* in the law of the LORD**, and in His law he meditates day and night. He shall be like a tree planted by the rivers of water, that brings forth its fruit in its season, whose leaf also shall not wither; and whatever he does shall prosper" (Psalm 1:2-3). These verses share two catalytic things (delighting and meditating in the law of the Lord) that create fruitfulness and prosperity. Delighting is to take pleasure in, and meditating is to mutter, muse or imagine. Something powerful happens in a life that becomes joyfully vocal about spiritual laws. Joshua was one of these when he was told, "This book of the law shall not depart from your mouth but you shall meditate in it day and night" (Joshua 1:8). It would seem that he and the psalmist knew something about God's laws that many miss.

"But his **delight** is in the law of the Lord." The person who revels in God's laws has gotten past seeing laws as rules and has entered into something joyous and revelatory. It is no longer about obeying to avoid punishment or to gain favor with God, but it is a bliss-filled discovery of the very nature of God through His laws. For example, as we delight in the law of generosity, we are led to the realization that He is the God of generosity. Or, as we joyfully ponder the power of honesty and truthfulness, we are brought to great spiritual delight by becoming fully convinced that God will always keep His word to us. Something wonderful happens when we intentionally take pleasure in the laws of the Spirit. It renews our minds and causes a "whatever he does shall prosper" experience. Now that's good news!

Truths About Spiritual Laws #20
Doesn't the Law Only Cause More Sin?
"The law entered that offense (sin) might abound" (Romans 5:20)

"*Is* the law then against the promises of God? Certainly not! For if there had been a law given which could have given life, truly righteousness would have been by the law" (Galatians 3:21). Even though the law supports the promises of God, we must realize that there is no life in trying to obey rules as the means to either Christian maturity or kingdom advancement. And not only is there no life in this, but being law-focused actually creates more sin. "Moreover the law entered that the offense might abound" Romans 5:20). The more we focus on our behavior, the worse our behavior will get.

The book of Romans sheds more light on this. "I was alive once without the law, but when the commandment came, sin revived and I died. And the commandment, which *was* to *bring* life, I found to *bring* death" (Romans 7:9-10). "I find then a law, that evil is present with me, the one who wills to do good. For I delight in the law of God according to the inward man. But I see another law in my members, warring against the law of my mind, and bringing me into captivity to the law of sin which is in my members. O wretched man that I am! Who will deliver me from this body of death? I thank God—through Jesus Christ our Lord" (Romans 7:21-24). Our inability to keep the rules (law) will lead us to truly find Jesus as the Christ (the powerful, anointed One). "Therefore the law was our tutor *to bring us* to Christ" (Galatians 3:24). As we consider these things, the question that must be asked is this: How can we emphasize the laws of the Spirit without creating an experience that works against us?

The answer to this is fourfold. First, we must resolve fully that salvation does not result from good works but only by grace through faith. (See Ephesians 2:8-9.) Secondly, we need to become (and remain) more beliefs'-focused than conduct-focused – realizing that empowering grace flows through believing truth. (See John 8:32; Galatians 3:1-5; 5:1-6.) Thirdly, we need to truly let the law lead us to Christ and have a dynamic encounter with His love, salvation and power— <u>where we have a relationship with Him instead of rule-keeping religion</u>. And, lastly, we are to prioritize and delight in the supernatural nature of God's laws instead of obeying rules. These four steps will not only help us to avoid having the law increase sin in us, but, more importantly, will help propel us to unlock true spiritual wisdom that will cause victory and abundance.

Truths About Spiritual Laws #21
The Spiritual Force of Revival

"But *His word* was in my heart like a burning fire" (Jeremiah 20:9)

I am a student of revivals. It stirs me to hear about the many powerful moves of the Holy Spirit throughout history. Hearing about past and present revivals keeps our spiritual expectation and spiritual fire at a high level. It kindles the belief that if God has done it anywhere, He can do it here. If He has done it anytime, He can do it now. And if it has been done through anyone, it can be done through us.

I am using the term "revival" to describe a time of heightened blessing and Holy Spirit activity in the church that builds momentum until it profoundly impacts the world. It is an awakening of seeing and understanding spiritual realities that have always been present but have been hidden through apathy and deception. Revival is a spiritual force (a fresh move of the Spirit) **that causes** spiritual hunger, salvations, the return of backsliders, miracles, encounters with God, family restoration, a heightened desire and empowerment to obey God's law, a decrease in crime, restitution, emotional healing and an increased love for Jesus.

The narrative in Acts 2 is an example of spiritual awakening and revival. The Spirit came with transforming power that caused common people to become extraordinary in Christ. They experienced a spiritual force from the unseen realm that transformed people's lives. Only the truly obstinate could seem to resist what was happening.

The experience of Acts has been repeated countless times in various ways. Just in the last 300 years, there have been powerful revivals that have sprung up in dark times. These include the Great Awakening (started in the 1730's), the Second Great Awakening (1790-1840's), the 1857 Worldwide Revival, the Welsh Revival of 1904 (which spread to India, China, Korea, Africa and America) and the Pentecostal Outpouring at Azusa Street in Los Angeles in the early 1900's. Each of these caused a miraculous spiritual momentum resulting in salvations, changed lives, powerful churches, decrease of social problems, healed families and a significantly greater belief in the importance of spiritual laws.

I share all these things so that you too will be a student of past revivals. I find it impossible to read about them without being revived myself (and believing for even greater things now and in the future). We don't wait for a corporate revival to experience personal revival, but we rejoice in the increased waves of global awakening that are coming!

Truths About Spiritual Laws #22
Overcoming the Debt Mentality

"Rather . . . than . . . enjoy the passing pleasures of sin " (Hebrews 11:25)

"By faith Moses, when he became of age, refused to be called the son of Pharaoh's daughter, choosing rather to suffer affliction with the people of God than to enjoy the **passing pleasures of sin,** . . . for **he looked to the reward**" (Hebrews 10:25). Moses chose to think and act with a long-term perspective in decision-making. Instead of having a debt-mentality (which sacrifices the future to meet current needs and desires), he said no to sin because he had already said yes to God and His ways.

Scripture does not deny that there can be a gratification in violating God's laws. It says there is an enjoyment of sin "for a season" (Hebrews 10:25 KJV). However, this pleasure is fleeting and deceptive.

As I consider this, I am reminded of a commercial I saw years ago for an automobile transmission repair company. The ad was urging car owners to come in for regular checkups and maintenance for the transmission. It said that if we did not do so, we risked having future major transmission problems that would cost much more than the checkup. The commercial's punch line was, "You can pay me now or you can pay me later." It was implied that if consumers did not pay the small fee for regular maintenance, they would eventually pay a great amount for major transmission repair.

"We can pay now or we can pay later" is a good phrase to remember as we seek to harness the power of spiritual laws to accomplish greater things for God (and to leave a blessing to those who come after us). It also speaks to us as we seek to avoid making decisions that we will regret and are hurtful to others. Wisdom sees through the momentary pleasure of disobeying God's spiritual laws and sees that there is a price to pay. Those who delay gratification may seem "uncool" and lagging behind in success, promotion, favor and blessing. The truth, however, is that they will reap the benefits of their good choices years later (when others unfortunately are reaping a harvest of negative seeds sown).

Yes, the debt-mentality mortgages the future for today. Its effects are clear in the area of finances, but it is also obvious in other areas of life such as relationships, honesty, attitude, work ethic, sexuality, spending time with God and time management. Like Moses, it takes faith to do the right thing when others are enjoying their season of pleasure in wrong choices. This can be especially challenging for teenagers and young adults, but God's grace is available to them and all of us in great ways.

Truths About Spiritual Laws #23
It is Impossible for Nothing to Happen
"For whatever a man sows, that he will also reap" (Galatians 6:7)

One of the most enlightening passages in the Bible is about spiritual laws. "Do not be deceived, God is not mocked; **for whatever a man sows, that he will also reap.** For he who sows to his flesh will of the flesh reap corruption, but he who sows to the Spirit will of the Spirit reap everlasting life. **And let us not grow weary while doing good, for in due season we shall reap if we do not lose heart**" (Galatians 6:7-9).

"Do not be deceived, God is not mocked." We must resist the deception that says that our lives are predestined in a specific direction and that our choices don't matter. We cannot embrace a belief system that thinks we are immune from either greatness or having severe consequences for our actions. We are told to not be deceived about the law of sowing and reaping for our lives. This reality should stir in us an excitement about our potential and a healthy fear of drifting from God and His ways.

"For whatever a man sows, that he will also reap" (Galatians 6:7 – see also Luke 6:36-38). This is a stunning truth. Our actions and beliefs are spiritual seeds that grow into a future harvest. If we sow friendship, we will reap friendship. If we give clothing to others, we will receive clothing. If we mistreat people, we will be mistreated. Farmers use this process in the natural, and people of wisdom take advantage of it in the spiritual. Indeed, **no matter where we are in life, there is a seed we can sow to positively change our future.**

"And let us not grow weary while doing good, for in due season we shall reap if we do not lose heart" (Galatians 6:9). The law of breakthrough comes from this verse and reveals that it is impossible for things to stay the same if we relentlessly sow to the spirit. We are told to not let weariness and a loss of heart stop us from sowing good seeds into the spirit realm. This implies that it will be normal for people to think that good choices are not doing any good. Circumstances that are not changing or getting worse will be screaming to the godly, "It is not working. There is no benefit to following God's ways. You need to quit. Even the godless are reaping a better harvest than you." This deception can sound convincing when we are worn out and disillusioned.

The time gap between sowing and reaping further challenges our beliefs, and, if we are not careful, we can move into doubt. We need to remember that just as a farmer must have faith that the planted seed will grow, we too must believe that our sown seed is growing in the unseen realm and will manifest in the visible. Yes, the persistent will see and release the goodness of God. Let's be one of them.

Truths About Spiritual Laws #24
Transitioning Into the Season of Increase
"Do not be deceived. God is not mocked" (Galatians 6:7)

Transitions are both exciting and scary. It is exciting because we are leaving some dead things and are on a path into new adventures. It is scary because the new season is filled with many uncertainties that challenge our faith. The good news is that God is a master at successfully leading His children through change and into a higher level of living.

When we are transitioning from the old to the new, we have to be aware that we will be living in both old and new during the transition time. (It won't be called transition any more when we are completely in the new!) As we first enter in this period of change, we will most likely be **experiencing** something like 80% old and 20% new in our lives. As we continue, the new will increase and the old decrease. This is important to understand.

Let's consider a farmer again. After he plants seed, he patiently waits for his new crops to grow. He knows that he is moving from being unfruitful to fruitful. His faith is not passive as he actively pulls weeds and waters the seeds planted. He does not lose heart because of the delay of seeing his harvest manifest.

We are spiritual farmers. If we walk in wisdom, we will deliberately, regularly and cheerfully plant seeds into the spirit realm. We too will have to deal with weeds that spring up during the time of waiting for our new harvest to come. These weeds are like thorny bushes that spring up and cause pain to us. They often result from seeds we have sown in the past that spring up during our time of transition. Unless we have a heavenly perspective, this can disillusion us and challenge our faith that things are changing.

Talking about these things is tricky. I don't want to create negative expectations, and I don't want to limit God's ability to immediately cancel bad seeds we have sown in the past. He is so merciful and has done this many times. (And as the kingdom keeps advancing, we will see blessings like supernatural debt cancellation increase more and more.) We rejoice in this, but we also tap into God's grace to face the weeds of frustrating circumstances that emerge in our transition time. He promises to meet all our needs "according to His riches in glory" (Philippians 4:19). His peace will "guard our hearts and minds in Christ Jesus" (Philippians 4:8). "And we know that all things work together for good to those who love God, to those who are the called according to *His* purpose" (Romans 8:28).

As we transition to a higher place in life, let's keep the faith in spite of negative circumstances and declare that our harvest is coming.

Truths About Spiritual Laws #25
Mad Spiritual Scientists Experimenting
"Above all that we ask or think" (Ephesians 3:20)

Aren't you glad that humans don't live in caves anymore, cook food over fire and make clothing out of animal skin? We have certainly advanced since those days, haven't we? We have all benefitted by dreamers and problem solvers who discovered superior ways of living.

Just think about recent advancements in life: landing a spacecraft on the moon, nuclear power, laser surgery, the Internet and the telephone. These improvements make us wonder what life is going to be like in fifty years. I have heard it said that technology is doubling every ten years. I don't know if this is true, but no one would deny that the last 150 years have brought unprecedented change through multiple inventions in such areas as transportation, communication, medicine and weaponry.

Many believe Daniel was told about the time we live in. "But you, Daniel, shut up the words, and seal the book until the time of the end; **many shall run to and fro, and knowledge shall increase**" (Daniel 12:4). There is definitely a great increase in travel and knowledge. It is also clear that there will be more and more technological advances that will be discovered. These will be done through people who experiment and take risks.

I believe that the phrase "knowledge shall increase" primarily refers to things in the spirit. It is the answer to Hosea 4:6: "My people are destroyed for lack of knowledge." The Bible calls us to advance and move from "faith to faith" (Romans 1:17) and "glory to glory" (2 Corinthians 3:18). We cannot fight today's battles with yesterday's revelation and spiritual weapons. Certainly, there are many things from the past that are foundational, but we must expect to discover higher ways of doing things.

Many Christians, unfortunately, are like Charles Duell, an official at the United States Patent Office, who said in 1899, "Everything that can be invented has been invented." We too often have a warped view of God's sovereignty that creates a "wait and see what God will do" passiveness.

We are called to not only be settlers, but also to be pioneers. We need to break out of routine and try new things. Yes, we value consistency in the basic disciplines of the faith, but higher spiritual ways and weapons won't be discovered unless someone is experimenting in God. We won't have people raised from the dead unless someone is thinking about how it happens (and actually prays for dead people). We won't have massive abundance unless someone is in a spiritual laboratory pondering and mixing various laws of the Spirit together. Why not you becoming that someone? Others will be glad you did.

Part Two

Examples of Spiritual Laws

EACH LAW IS ADDRESSED IN FIVE WAYS:

1. **This law is revealed in the Bible in passages such as . . .** – Scripture is the foundation for the law's truth.
2. **This law will work for us to cause increase and blessing if . . .** – Practical wisdom is given concerning how to activate the law into our lives.
3. **This law will work against us to restrict and impoverish us . . .** – We are urged to avoid the foolishness of violating the laws of the Spirit.
4. **This law will bring us into a greater intimacy with God because . . .** – Each law reveals an aspect of God's nature to be discovered.
5. **I delight in this law by joyfully declaring** . . . – When we bridle our words, we bridle our whole body. (See James 3:2.) Our words are a rudder to take us toward this law being lived out in our lives. (See James 3:3-5.)

Law of the Spirit #1
The Law of Giving and Generosity
"Give and it will be given to you" (Luke 6:38)

This law is revealed in the Bible in passages such as: "Give, and it will be given to you: good measure, pressed down, shaken together, and running over will be put into your bosom. For with the same measure that you use, it will be measured back to you" (Luke 6:38). "But this *I say:* He who sows sparingly will also reap sparingly, and he who sows bountifully will also reap bountifully" (2 Corinthians 9:6). "Honor the LORD with your possessions, and with the firstfruits of all your increase; so your barns will be filled with plenty, and your vats will overflow with new wine" (Proverbs 3:9-10). "For whatever a man sows, that he will also reap" (Galatians 6:7). "God loves a cheerful giver" (2 Corinthians 9:7).

This law will work for us and cause increase and blessing if we are generous and give good things to others. Whatever we give away will become a deposit into the spirit realm that will be returned in like kind to us and/or to our descendents. If we give encouragement, we will receive encouragement. If we give friendship, we will receive friendship. If we give money, we will receive money. And we will receive back bountifully if we have given bountifully. Intentional giving brings blessing to us.

This law will work against us to restrict and impoverish us if we give sparingly or not at all. This will greatly limit our future resources. Also, we will have problems if we do hurtful things to others because that which is given will come back to us (i.e. criticism, abuse, impatience, etc.).

This law will bring us into a greater intimacy with God because it helps us to discover that He is extremely generous to us. "For God so loved the world that He gave His only begotten Son, that whoever believes in Him should not perish but have everlasting life" (John 3:16). The "measure" that God used to express His love and value for us was His best (His only Son). As we worship Him as the Generous One, we realize that He (like a loving parent) wants to lavish good things on His children. (See Matthew 7:11.) This revelation eradicates the lie that He is stingy or that we are unworthy of being blessed.

I delight in this law by joyfully declaring: God is generous and so am I. I am a cheerful giver and receive back a great harvest as a result. I plant seeds for my future provision through generous gifts to others. I am discovering how generous my God is, and this is changing my life.

Law of the Spirit #2
The Law of Kingdom Priorities
"Seek first the kingdom and His righteousness" (Matthew 6:33)

This law is revealed in the Bible in passages such as: "You shall have no other gods before Me" (Exodus 20:3). "Seek first the kingdom of God and His righteousness, and all these things shall be added to you" (Matthew 6:33). "*You looked for much, but indeed it came to little; and when you brought it home, I blew it away. Why?*' says the LORD of hosts. 'Because of My house that *is in* ruins, while every one of you runs to his own house'" (Haggai 1:9).

This law will work for us and cause increase and blessing if we make God our first priority in life. "Therefore do not worry, saying, 'What shall we eat?' or 'What shall we drink?' or 'What shall we wear?' . . . For your heavenly Father knows that you need all these things. But seek first the kingdom of God and His righteousness, and all these things shall be added to you" (Matthew 6:31-33). This mighty promise reinforces the first of the Ten Commandments (the *very first* spiritual law) of putting God first. It causes a pipeline of provision to be directed at those who love Jesus first, who believe they are righteous in Him and who have dedicated their lives for kingdom advancement.

This law will work against us to restrict and impoverish us if we have other things ahead of our relationship with Jesus. As the people of Haggai's day discovered, blessing and protection decrease when other things replace God and His house as our first life priority. The people of Haggai's time were not blessed because of this. They were told, "Consider your ways! You have sown much, and bring in little . . . And he who earns wages, Earns wages *to put* into a bag with holes" (Haggai 1:6). Their problem was not a poor work ethic or unfriendly weather patterns, but a violation of a spiritual law. The solution was to prioritize God and His kingdom.

This law will bring us into a greater intimacy with God because it helps us to discover that I am His number one priority. He loved me and pursued me when I had no heart for Him. "But God demonstrates His own love toward us, in that while we were still sinners, Christ died for us" (Romans 5:8). The father of the prodigal in Luke 15 reveals that I am first on God's mind. "And he arose and came to his father. But when he was still a great way off, his father saw him and had compassion, **and ran** and fell on his neck and kissed him" (Luke 15:20).

I delight in this law by joyfully declaring: I am God's first priority, and I worship Him as mine. As I place Him first in all I do, there is a supernatural abundant release of protection and provision to me.

Law of the Spirit #3
The Law of Honesty and Integrity

"You shall not bear false witness against your neighbor" (Exodus 20:16)

This law is revealed in the Bible in passages such as: "He who walks with integrity walks securely" (Proverbs 10:9). "The truthful lip shall be established forever" (Proverbs 12:9). "The righteous *man* walks in his integrity; His children *are* blessed after him" (Proverbs 20:7). "You shall not bear false witness against your neighbor" (Exodus 20:16). "He who has a deceitful heart finds no good, And he who has a perverse tongue falls into evil" (Proverbs 17:20).

This law will work for us and cause increase and blessing if we become a person of honesty and integrity. Those who walk in truthfulness create a long-term blessing for their descendents and themselves. In the small sample of verses above, we can see that sowing honesty and integrity will bring about security (safety), establishment (longevity) and blessing for the lineage of the honest one. It is a marvelous spiritual law that can be intentionally activated and increased through such things as: by following through on what we say we are going to do, being honest in "little things," by not participating in gossip and by being honest with God (and at least one other person) about who we really are and what is happening in our lives.

This law will work against us to restrict and impoverish us if we become a person who lies and cheats to supposedly move forward in life. The story of Ananias and Sapphira in Acts 5 is a dramatic example of protection being completely removed because of dishonesty. We don't see this instant death today, but life and blessing will slowly die when integrity is abandoned because of a belief that "the end justifies the means."

This law will bring us into a greater intimacy with God because it helps us to discover that God keeps His word. We rejoice in verses that tell us that He is the ultimate promise keeper. "In hope of eternal life which God, who cannot lie, promised before time began" (Titus 1:2). "It *is* impossible for God to lie" (Hebrews 6:18). "God *is* not a man, that He should lie" (Numbers 23:19). We worship Him as the Truthful One. We also realize that He is not only truthful, but He is the Truth. (See John 14:6.) Hallelujah.

I delight in this law by joyfully declaring: God is honest and full of integrity, and so am I. My life is leaving an inheritance of blessing and protection for my descendents because I am walking in truth.

Law of the Spirit #4
The Law of Effort and Diligence

"The plans of the diligent lead surely to plenty" (Proverbs 21:5)

This law is revealed in the Bible in passages such as: "The plans of the diligent *lead* surely to plenty, but *those of* everyone *who is* hasty, surely to poverty (Proverbs 21:5). "But the soul of the diligent shall be made rich (Proverbs 13:4). "He who is slothful in his work is a brother to him who is a great destroyer" (Proverbs 18:9). "The way of the lazy *man is* like a hedge of thorns, but the way of the upright *is* a highway" (Proverbs 15:19). "He who has a slack hand becomes poor, but the hand of the diligent makes rich" (Proverbs 10:4). "And let us not grow weary while doing good, for in due season we shall reap if we do not lose heart" (Galatians 6:9).

This law will work for us and cause increase and blessing if we become a person with a strong work ethic. Many doors of blessing will open for us through effort, hard work and diligence. Yes, we want to avoid becoming a "work-a-holic" (or thinking that works are more important than beliefs), but we cannot deny the vital importance of good work habits that are characterized through diligence, meticulousness, conscientiousness, thoroughness, attentiveness and carefulness. These attributes become a powerful deposit into the spirit that will create a future release of abundance and protection. Indeed, Thomas Jefferson said, "I'm a great believer in luck, and I find the harder I work the more I have of it." Remember the difference between try and triumph is a little umph.

This law will work against us to restrict and impoverish us if we allow ourselves to become slothful, lazy, idle, apathetic, passive and a lover of sleep. Proverbs 18:9 reveals that "He who is slothful in his work is a brother to him who is a great destroyer." Those who do not develop dynamic work habits actually destroy the potential of great blessing being released; and, as a result, will cause poverty to increase and be solidified.

This law will bring us into a greater intimacy with God because it helps us to discover that God is always working on my behalf. "And we know that all things work together for good to those who love God, to those who are the called according to *His* purpose" (Romans 8:28). We worship Him as the One who miraculously works everything into good as I love Him and dedicate my life to the call of His purpose for me.

I delight in this law by joyfully declaring: I am a hard worker. I am diligent. I do small things in a great way. I am a person of excellence. I finish what I start. Great increase is ahead because of my powerful work ethic.

Law of the Spirit #5
The Law of Humility

"God resists the proud, but gives grace to the humble" (James 4:6)

This law is revealed in the Bible in passages such as: "Before destruction the heart of a man is haughty, and before honor *is* humility" (Proverbs 18:12). "By humility *and* the fear of the LORD *are* riches and honor and life" (Proverbs 23:4). "A man's pride will bring him low, but the humble in spirit will retain honor" (Proverbs 29:3). "God resists the proud, but gives grace to the humble" (James 4:6). "Therefore humble yourselves under the mighty hand of God, that He may exalt you in due time" (I Peter 5:6). "Let this mind be in you which was also in Christ Jesus, who, being in the form of God, did not consider it robbery to be equal with God, but made Himself of no reputation, taking the form of a bondservant, *and* coming in the likeness of men. And being found in appearance as a man, He humbled Himself and became obedient to *the point of* death, even the death of the cross" (Philippians 2:5-8). "Whoever exalts himself will be humbled, and he who humbles himself will be exalted" (Matthew 23:12).

This law will work for us to cause increase and blessing if we embrace humility with its attributes of being grateful, teachable, accountable, honorable and dependent on God. True humility makes a deposit in the spirit realm that will bring a harvest of honor, riches, grace, exaltation, life and more. Humility not only causes favor with God but also with people. (Please note: Biblical humility is not self-deprecating or self-critical.)

This law will work against us to restrict and impoverish us if we reject humility and walk in arrogance with its attitudes of ungratefulness, stubbornness, prayerlessness, dishonor and superiority. Pride blocks the flow of grace into our lives and produces destruction and future humbling circumstances.

This law will bring us into a greater intimacy with God because it helps us to discover that God has demonstrated in Jesus the ultimate act of humility – humbling Himself to bring salvation and life to earth. Even though He is all-powerful, He restrains His power and, in essence, submits Himself to the free will of man. "The Son of Man did not come to be served, but to serve, and to give His life a ransom for many" (Mark 10:45). We worship Him as the One who has come to serve our deepest needs.

I delight in this law by joyfully declaring: I am a humble person. I am teachable and honorable. I am thankful because the good things in my life come from the goodness of God and the help of others. My humility causes me to receive empowering grace and success.

Law of the Spirit #6
The Law of Association
"He who walks with wise *men* will be wise" (Proverbs 13:20)

This law is revealed in the Bible in passages such as: "He who walks with wise *men* will be wise, but the companion of fools will be destroyed" (Proverbs 13:20). "Do not be deceived: 'Evil company corrupts good habits'" (I Corinthians 15:33). "And everyone *who was* in distress, everyone *who was* in debt, and everyone *who was* discontented gathered to him (David)" (I Samuel 22:2). "Now when they saw the boldness of Peter and John, and perceived that they were uneducated and untrained men, they marveled. And they realized that they had been with Jesus" (Acts 4:13). "Now Joshua the son of Nun was full of the spirit of wisdom, for Moses had laid his hands on him" (Deuteronomy 34:9). "When Solomon was old . . . his wives turned his heart after other gods" (I Kings 11:4).

This law will work for us and cause increase and blessing if we intentionally align ourselves with people who are ahead of us in the things of God and life. The "3-D People" of I Samuel 22 (those in debt, distress and discontent) became the mighty men of David in 2 Samuel 23 because of their association and commitment to David. Likewise, the dysfunctional disciples in the gospels became world changers because of their covenant relationship with Jesus. We too can accelerate our success in life by partnering with people of wisdom and victory.

This law will work against us to restrict and impoverish us if our main relationships are with those who do not honor God or His spiritual laws. Scripture admonishes us to avoid being misled concerning this. "Do not be deceived: 'Evil company corrupts good habits'" (I Corinthians 15:33).

This law will bring us into a greater intimacy with God because it helps us to discover that He is the greatest association that we can have, and that we will become like Him (and become blessed) by being in His presence. The untrained disciples became astoundingly like Jesus through being with Him. Moses' face shone because He also was with God. (See Exodus 34:35.) The disciples and Moses illustrate the reality of 2 Corinthians 3:18. "We all, with unveiled face, beholding as in a mirror the glory of the Lord, **are being transformed** into the same image from glory to glory."

I delight in this law by joyfully declaring: I walk with the wise. I am committed to people who are more blessed than I am. I have renounced unhealthy relationships. I spend so much time in God's presence that it is obvious to others that I have been with Jesus.

Law of the Spirit #7
The Law of Faithfulness in Small Things
"A faithful man will abound with blessings" (Proverbs 28:20)

This law is revealed in the Bible in passages such as: "He who *is* faithful in *what is* least is faithful also in much; and he who is unjust in *what is* least is unjust also in much" (Luke 16:10). "A faithful man will abound with blessings, but he who hastens to be rich will not go unpunished" (Proverbs 28:20). "Well *done*, good and faithful servant; you were faithful over a few things, I will make you ruler over many things. Enter into the joy of your lord" (Matthew 25:21). "Then came the first, saying, 'Master, your mina has earned ten minas.' And he said to him, 'Well *done*, good servant; because you were faithful in a very little, have authority over ten cities'" (Luke 19:16-17). "For who has despised the day of small things?" (Zechariah 4:10).

This law will work for us to cause increase and blessing if we understand that faithfulness with today's assignments and responsibilities is the doorway into greater blessing and privilege in the days ahead. The things in our lives now (possessions, finances, jobs, ministries, relationships, etc.) are the training ground to build faithfulness so that we can be entrusted with more in the future.

This law will work against us to restrict and impoverish us if we are not faithful with the small things in our lives now and wait until a supposedly better time to become excellent and consistent. In the Parable of the Talents, the individual who received the one talent did not see it as his "test" to determine whether he was ready for more. (See Matthew 25:24-25.) He let fear, laziness and a distorted image of God neutralize his risk-taking and enthusiasm for his current opportunities. We cannot let this happens to us.

This law will bring us into a greater intimacy with God because it causes us to discover that He is faithful and true to us. We worship Him as the Faithful One! "If we are faithless, He remains faithful; He cannot deny Himself" (2 Timothy 2:13). "Know therefore that the LORD your God is God; He is the faithful God, keeping His covenant of love to a thousand generations . . ." (Deuteronomy 7:9). We lift our hands and say, "We love you Lord! We love Your faithfulness to us. As we behold your faithfulness, we become faithful, too."

I delight in this law by joyfully declaring: I am excited about doing little things well. Indeed, I do small things in a great way. I am a person of responsibility, excellence, thoroughness and enthusiasm; and I do more than is expected. I am a faithful person who loves my faithful God. I rejoice in knowing there are "greater things" in my future because I am faithful today.

Law of the Spirit #8
The Law of Spiritual Inheritance

"A good man leaves an inheritance to his children's children" (Prov. 13:22)

This law is revealed in the Bible in passages such as: " . . . visiting the iniquity of the fathers upon the children to the third and fourth *generations* of those who hate Me, but showing mercy to thousands, to those who love Me and keep My commandments" (Exodus 20:5-6). "Therefore the LORD said to Solomon . . . 'I will surely tear the kingdom away from you . . . Nevertheless I will not do it in your days, for the sake of your father David" (1 Kings 11:11-12). "Now Joshua . . . was full of the spirit of wisdom, for Moses had laid his hands on him" (Deuteronomy 34:9). "I (Nehemiah) . . . confess the sins of the children of Israel which we have sinned against You" (Nehemiah 1:6). "He who receives a prophet in the name of a prophet shall receive a prophet's reward" (Matthew 10:41).

This law will work for us to cause increase and blessing if we by faith "pull on" the good deposits made in the spirit realm by our ancestors. Honoring God's laws creates blessings to "thousands" of generations. (See Exodus 20:6.) Generational blessings are more powerful and long lasting than generational curses. Renouncing generational curses may be a good step, but it's more important to have the Spirit reveal to us the force of generational blessings. We can also receive inheritances from key people who are in our lives now. Just as Joshua received wisdom because Moses laid his hands on him, we can receive things we have not worked for. Matthew 10:41 gives insight on how to receive this kind of inheritance. "He who receives a prophet in the name of a prophet receives a prophet's reward." The inheritance (reward) comes when we do not allow offense to cause us to dishonor a person's gift. (See Mark 6:1-6.)

This law will work against us to restrict and impoverish us if we don't believe that Jesus became a curse for us so that we can be free from such things as generational curses. Yes, we may need to take specific actions (forgiving, seeking forgiveness, renouncing, restitution, etc.) to help eliminate the root of the curse in the spiritual realm, but believing in and receiving the finished work of the cross is the most important thing we can do to be free from generational curses.

This law will bring us into a greater intimacy with God because it causes us to discover that we are already joint heirs with Christ Jesus of all that He deserves as God's only Son. (See Romans 8:17.) More importantly, we realize that God Himself is our inheritance. Jesus has opened up a way for us to be with Him in glorious intimacy forever!

I delight in this law by joyfully declaring: I receive right now my generational blessings from Jesus and from my ancestors.

Law of the Spirit #9
The Law of Caring for the Poor
"He who gives to the poor will not lack" (Proverbs 28:27)

This law is revealed in the Bible in passages such as: "He who has pity on the poor lends to the LORD, and He will pay back what he has given" (Proverbs 19:7). "He who gives to the poor will not lack, but he who hides his eyes will have many curses" (Proverbs 28:27). "The king who judges the poor with truth, his throne will be established forever" (Proverbs 29:14). "*If* you extend your soul to the hungry and satisfy the afflicted soul, then your light shall dawn in the darkness . . . The LORD will guide you continually, and satisfy your soul in drought, and strengthen your bones; you shall be like a watered garden, and like a spring of water, whose waters do not fail" (Isaiah 58:10-11). "He who has a generous eye will be blessed, for he gives of his bread to the poor" (Proverbs 22:9).

This law will work for us to cause increase and blessing if we dedicate our lives to help those who are poor in spirit, money, shelter, food, emotional health, physical health, identity beliefs, integrity, relationship skills, love, hope, faith, and other areas of life. Those who have compassion on the poor will be a blessing to them and will become blessed themselves. We especially want to find practical ways to help those who are struggling to have the basic necessities of life. God's promises for doing this are marvelous (paying us back, blessed longevity, light during dark times, guidance, continual satisfaction, strength, health, unusual vibrancy and vitality).

This law will work against us to restrict and impoverish us if we "close our eyes" to needs around us and do not develop a heart for the poor. Selfishness blocks the flow of blessing into our lives. We cannot just accumulate for ourselves, but we are created to become a blessing to those who need what we have. If we don't adopt and maintain this mindset, the flow of blessing will dry up.

This law will bring us into a greater intimacy with God because it causes us to discover that He really loves us and constantly wants to give to us in the poor areas of our lives. What makes this revelation even more marvelous is the realization that God does not lack anything where I am poor. I can worship Him as the one who gives generously to the poor.

I delight in this law by joyfully declaring: I have compassion for the poor. My life is dedicated to help the poor in spirit, poor in possessions and poor in life skills to come out of poverty and into blessing. I have wisdom concerning when to give and when not to give. I have divine strategies to help eliminate the root of people's poverty. I also am receiving revelation of God's heart for the poor (including me) and how to see His abundance released to others and me.

Law of the Spirit #10
The Law of Words
"Death and life are in the power of the tongue" (Proverbs 18:21)

This law is revealed in the Bible in passages such as: "A man will be satisfied with good by the fruit of *his* mouth" (Proverbs 12:14). "Death and life *are* in the power of the tongue, and those who love it will eat its fruit" (Proverbs 18:21). "If anyone does not stumble in word, he *is* a perfect man, able also to bridle the whole body. Indeed, we put bits in horses' mouths that they may obey us, and we turn their whole body. Look also at ships: although they are so large and are driven by fierce winds, they are turned by a very small rudder wherever the pilot desires. Even so the tongue . . ." (James 3:2-5). "Let no corrupt word proceed out of your mouth, but what is good for necessary edification, that it may impart grace to the hearers" (Ephesians 4:29). "By the blessing of the upright the city is exalted, but it is overthrown by the mouth of the wicked" (Proverbs 11:11). "Out of the same mouth proceed blessing and cursing. My brethren, these things ought not to be so" (James 3:10).

This law will work for us to cause increase and blessing if we love to speak words of life that are in agreement with God's promises and His perspective. Scripture reveals that good words will satisfy us, cause fruitfulness, bring control to our lives, impart grace to the hearers, exalt cities and direct the course that our lives are going. Those who intentionally "speak life" will become a creative force of blessing for others and themselves. It is one of the most powerful spiritual laws in existence because we understand that for something to happen, something must be spoken.

This law will work against us to restrict and impoverish us if we are in the habit of verbalizing negative conclusions that are contrary to God's promises. We don't deny bad circumstances, nor do we walk in fear of talking about problems, but we must know that decline and death are frequently "in the power of the tongue." Too many people have placed word curses on themselves, others and their circumstances because they don't know how powerful they are.

This law will bring us into a greater intimacy with God because we will discover that God is a speaker of life over me. He sent His Word in the person of Jesus to heal us. (See Psalm 107:20; John 1:1-3, 14.) We worship and adore Him as the One who is the unceasing speaker of His thoughts toward me—that I have a future and a hope, that I am loved, etc.

I delight in this law by joyfully declaring: I am a speaker of life. My words positively set the course of my life and those connected to me. The word curses of the past have ceased and have been cut off, and now I impart abounding grace to all who hear my words (including me).

Law of the Spirit #11
The Law of Forgiveness
"Forgive, and you will be forgiven" (Luke 6:37)

This law is revealed in the Bible in passages such as: "Judge not, and you shall not be judged. Condemn not, and you shall not be condemned. Forgive, and you will be forgiven" (Luke 6:37). "Looking carefully lest anyone fall short of the grace of God; lest any root of bitterness springing up cause trouble, and by this many become defiled" (Hebrews 12:15). "Jesus said, 'Father, forgive them, for they do not know what they do'" (Luke 23:34). "If you have anything against anyone, forgive him, that your Father in heaven may also forgive you your trespasses" (Mark 11:25). "Blessed *are* the merciful, for they shall obtain mercy" (Matthew 5:7). "If you forgive the sins of any, they are forgiven them; if you retain the *sins* of any, they are retained" (John 20:23).

This law will work for us to cause increase and blessing if we know that forgiveness and mercy are powerful spiritual weapons that create "open heavens" over lives so they can more freely receive the things of God. Jesus' words of forgiveness over those who crucified Him were instrumental in the 3,000 being saved on the day of Pentecost. (See Luke 23:24, Acts 2:41.) This is further illustrated when Stephen forgave those stoning him, "Lord, do not charge them with this sin" (Acts 7:60). Saul of Tarsus was one of the main targets of Stephen's forgiveness – and Saul had a life-altering encounter as a result. Forgiveness and mercy indeed help those we forgive, but it also causes a greater open heaven over ourselves. Greater measures of forgiveness and mercy will manifest to us (with its benefits) as we forgive and extend mercy.

This law will work against us to restrict and impoverish us if we refuse to forgive those who hurt us. Bitterness imprisons and torments our lives., and it defiles (contaminates) our environments. (See Matthew 18:21-35 and Hebrews 12:15.) Forgiveness does not mean we don't have boundaries in relationships, but it does mean we release people from our judgment of their actions.

This law will bring us into a greater intimacy with God because it will cause us to discover that we are forgiven much. Jesus spoke of this when He answered Simon the Pharisee's condemnation of a woman who poured perfume on His feet, "Therefore I say to you, her sins, *which are* many, are forgiven, for she loved much. But to whom little is forgiven, *the same* loves little" (Luke 7:47). As we receive greater revelation of how much we are forgiven, we worship and increasingly love Him as the Forgiving One.

I delight in this law by joyfully declaring: I have been forgiven much, and I love much. One of my chief spiritual weapons is forgiveness. Heaven opens over lives, regions and me because I intentionally and proactively forgive.

Law of the Spirit #12
The Law of Sexual Purity
"Flee sexual immorality" (I Corinthians 6:18)

This law is revealed in the Bible in passages such as: "Male and female He created them. Then God blessed them, and God said to them, 'Be fruitful and multiply; fill the earth and subdue it'" (Genesis 1:27-28). "Therefore a man shall leave his father and mother and be joined to his wife, and they shall become one flesh. And they were both naked, the man and his wife, and were not ashamed" (Genesis 2:24-25). "Blessed *are* the pure in heart, for they shall see God" (Matthew 5:8). "You shall not commit adultery" (Exodus 20:14). "Now the works of the flesh are evident, which are: adultery, fornication, uncleanness, lewdness . . ." (Galatians 5:22). "Flee sexual immorality. Every sin that a man does is outside the body, but he who commits sexual immorality sins against his own body" (I Corinthians 6:18).

This law will work for us to cause increase and blessing if we realize that sexual intimacy is the glue of unity between a man and woman after marriage. This spiritual and physical oneness creates possibilities in life that are not available in any other earthly relationship—and these possibilities extend far beyond the great mandate to be fruitful and multiply. Also, strong families are the basic building block of a strong society—with the marriage covenant as its foundation. Societal blessing increases as families get stronger—and sexual fidelity (in thought and deed) is a basic ingredient to healthy families.

This law will work against us to restrict and impoverish us if we engage in sexual activity outside of the boundaries God has established. The lack of self-control regarding sex creates a whole host of immediate problems (curses) for individuals and nations (i.e. diseases, rape, molestations, the breakup of families, fatherless children, human sex trafficking, emotional suffering, abortions, sex addictions, etc.). The breakdown in sexuality is also a main cause for the deterioration of spiritual protection over a people. **Please note two things:** 1) Spiritual heart change (not laws and rules) is the key to seeing change in this vital area of life, and 2) God can restore and heal us of any poor sexual choices of the past.

This law will bring us into a greater intimacy with God because the sexual union exemplifies the bliss-filled and life-giving spiritual encounters that we must have with Him for true revival to be birthed and sustained. Just as Mary was impregnated with God's solution for mankind, we too are to conceive and birth spiritual revival that results from passionate and powerful encounters with God.

I delight in this law by joyfully declaring: I live a life of sexual purity. I am healed of past events that warped my sexuality. I am a person who experiences the deepest level of intimacy with God and people.

Law of the Spirit #13
The Law of Blessing Israel

"I will bless those who bless you . . . curse him who curses you" (Genesis 12:3)

This law is revealed in the Bible in passages such as: "Now the LORD had said to Abram: 'Get out of your country, from your family and from your father's house, to a land that I will show you. I will make you a great nation; I will bless you and make your name great; and you shall be a blessing. I will bless those who bless you, and I will curse him who curses you; and in you all the families of the earth shall be blessed'" (Genesis 12:1-3). "Pray for the peace of Jerusalem: 'May they prosper who love you. Peace be within your walls, prosperity within your palaces'" (Psalm 122:6-7). "The LORD did not set His love on you nor choose you (Israel) because you were more in number than any other people, for you were the least of all peoples; but because the LORD loves you, and because He would keep the oath which He swore to your fathers . . ." (Deuteronomy 7:7-8). "On the same day the LORD made a covenant with Abram, saying: 'To your descendants I have given this land, from the river of Egypt to the great river, the River Euphrates'" (Genesis 15:18). "Moses My servant is dead. Now therefore, arise, go over this Jordan, you and all this people, to the land which I am giving to them—the children of Israel . . . From the wilderness and this Lebanon as far as the great river, the River Euphrates, all the land of the Hittites, and to the Great Sea toward the going down of the sun, shall be your territory" (Joshua 1:2-4).

This law will work for us to cause increase and blessing if we bless Israel and the Jewish people. Honoring Israel is one component of walking in the wisdom that releases great blessing. God made a special covenant with the Jews and their land, and He will not break His promise. Of course, we cannot use our esteeming of the Jews as an excuse to mistreat other people, but it is vital to know that powerful spiritual laws are activated by attitudes and behavior toward the people of Israel.

This law will work against us to restrict and impoverish us if our actions and words become a restriction to Israel and the Jewish people's success.

This law will bring us into a greater intimacy with God because we discover that God keeps His covenants and promises with His people. Even if we are unfaithful, He remains faithful. (See 2 Timothy 2:13.)

I delight in this law by joyfully declaring: I love and bless Israel in various ways. As a result, I am blessed tremendously.

Law of the Spirit #14
The Law of Covenants

"Then Jonathan and David made a covenant" (1 Samuel 18:3)

This law is revealed in the Bible in passages such as: "And it happened at the end of three days, after they had made a covenant with them (the Gibeonites), that they heard that they *were* their neighbors who dwelt near them . . . But the children of Israel did not attack them, because the rulers of the congregation had sworn to them by the LORD God of Israel . . . Then all the rulers said to all the congregation, 'We have sworn to them by the LORD God of Israel . . . We will let them live, lest wrath be upon us because of the oath which we swore to them'" (Joshua 9:16-20). "Now there was a famine in the days of David for three years, year after year; and David inquired of the LORD. And the LORD answered, '*It is* because of Saul and *his* bloodthirsty house, because he killed the Gibeonites'" (2 Samuel 21:1).

This law will work for us to cause increase and blessing if we make promises and commitments and then follow through on them (especially covenant commitments). A covenant relationship is based upon shared commitments. It usually involves promises, obligations and some kind of ritual to begin. It was illustrated in Joshua 9 when the Israelites kept a commitment (even though it was based on deception). They desired to walk in blessing and not "wrath" (which results when protection decreases through wrong moral choices). The quality of our lives is based on the quality of our commitments. A quick consideration of the people we know will reveal the benefits of keeping commitments to such things as family, moral choices, work, etc. These "promise keepers" not only avoid many pitfalls in life but also have the spiritual force of blessing on them.

This law will work against us to restrict and impoverish us if we avoid making commitments or if we are not a person who follows through on what we say (especially covenant commitments).

This law will bring us into a greater intimacy with God because we will discover that God has made a covenant commitment to us that He will not break. Indeed, He has made a "New Covenant" with us that reveals His total and eternal commitment to our absolute highest good. I worship Him as the Glorious Covenant Keeper and Promise Keeper to me.

I delight in this law by joyfully declaring: I have great wisdom about who I make commitments to. Once I have done so, I have a great grace to follow through on those things. I also rejoice in the new covenant that I have with God. I am receiving daily revelation of the wonders of this glorious relationship.

Law of the Spirit #15
The Law of Sabbath Rest
"Remember the Sabbath day" (Exodus 20:8)

This law is revealed in the Bible in passages such as: "Remember the Sabbath day, to keep it holy. Six days you shall labor and do all your work, but the seventh day *is* the Sabbath of the LORD your God. *In it* you shall do no work: you, nor your son, nor your daughter, nor your male servant, nor your female servant, nor your cattle, nor your stranger who *is* within your gates. For *in* six days the LORD made the heavens and the earth, the sea, and all that *is* in them, and rested the seventh day. Therefore the LORD blessed the Sabbath day and hallowed it" (Exodus 20:8-11). "So let no one judge you in food or in drink, or regarding a festival or a new moon or sabbaths, which are a shadow of things to come, but the substance is of Christ" (Colossians 2:16-17). "There remains therefore a rest for the people of God. For he who has entered His rest has himself also ceased from his works as God *did* from His" (Hebrews 4:9-10).

This law will work for us to cause increase and blessing if we live a life that prioritizes rest (both spiritually and physically). Just as tithing does not make sense to the natural mind as a means for increase, resting seems ridiculous as a means to accomplish more. God Himself is our example of setting aside a specific day to rest and replenish. He commanded the Jews in the Old Testament to take one day a week to take a break from work and focus on Him. In the New Covenant, we do not legalistically keep one specific day as a Sabbath, but we should adopt the Sabbath principle of devoting time (ideally one day a week) to relax and refuel physically, emotionally, relationally and spiritually. This habit will help us enter into the spiritual rest of Hebrews 4 that results from a deep trust in God. The Sabbath rest principle creates blessings for those who value it.

This law will work against us to restrict and impoverish us if we become a work-a-holic who ignores setting aside time to rest, relax, "soak" in God, focus on relationships and have fun. We will have unnecessary spiritual resistance if we do not commit to a clear set of priorities that includes experiencing Sabbath rest.

This law will bring us into a greater intimacy with God because we will discover that God is not stressed and is at rest Himself. We worship Him as the One at rest, and we receive rest for our own souls.

I delight in this law by joyfully declaring: I prioritize times of rest, relaxation and replenishment for my spirit, soul and body. As a result, I receive blessing from the spirit realm for longevity and success.

Law of the Spirit #16
The Law of Personal Identity
"We were like grasshoppers in our own sight" (Numbers 13:33)

This law is revealed in the Bible in passages such as: "They gave . . . a bad report of the land which they had spied out, saying, 'The land . . . devours its inhabitants, and all the people whom we saw in it *are* men of *great* stature. There we saw the giants . . . and we were like grasshoppers in our own sight, and so we were in their sight" (Numbers 13:32-33). "For as he thinks in his heart, so *is* he" (Proverbs 23:7). "Therefore . . . making mention of you in my prayers: that . . . God . . . may give to you the spirit of wisdom and revelation in the knowledge of Him, the eyes of your understanding being enlightened; that you may know what is the hope of His calling, what are the riches of the glory of His inheritance in the saints, and what *is* the exceeding greatness of His power toward us who believe, according to the working of His mighty power" (Ephesians 1:15-19).

This law will work for us to cause increase and blessing if we believe who God says we are–even if it does not agree with our experience or what others have told us. Just as the Angel of the Lord needed to convince the great deliverer Gideon that he was truly a "mighty man of valor" (Judges 6:12), we too need the eyes of our understanding enlightened to really know our true identity in Christ. Abram created an avalanche of blessing when at age 99 he discovered a way to believe he was a "father of a multitude" when it looked utterly hopeless. (See Genesis 17:4-8; Romans 4:16-22.) We have even greater possibilities than Abraham to release blessing (by believing God's promise instead of our experience) because we live in a better covenant with better promises. (See Heb. 8:6.)

This law will work against us to restrict and impoverish us if we, like the ten spies in Numbers 13, see ourselves as insignificant and as victims. This false conclusion of our identity will create a misdiagnosis of our circumstances, which will lead to limitation and defeat. As we think in our heart, "so are we" (Proverbs 23:7). If we think we are weak, we are weak. If we think we are a sinner (instead of a saint), we will "sin by faith" because of that belief system. If we think we are unworthy to be blessed, it will be nearly impossible for us to receive and increase the blessing needed to increase our talents and make a difference–for "we do not see things as they are. We see them as we are" (The Talmud).

This law will bring us into a greater intimacy with God because we will discover that He believes in us much more than we believe in ourselves. He is our prime source for encouragement, love and affirmation.

I delight in this law by joyfully declaring: I am who God says I am. I am loved, strong, evangelistic, organized, loving, self-controlled, a miracle worker and wise. I pull in resources and change environments as a result.

Law of the Spirit #17
The Law of Unity and Agreement

"Again I say to you that if two of you agree on earth " (Mathew 18:19)

This law is revealed in the Bible in passages such as: "And the LORD said, 'Indeed the people are one and they all have one language, and this is what they begin to do; now nothing that they propose to do will be withheld from them'" (Genesis 11:6). "Behold, how good and how pleasant *it is* for brethren to dwell together in unity! *It is* like the precious oil upon the head, running down on the beard, the beard of Aaron, running down on the edge of his garments . . . for there the LORD commanded the blessing—life forevermore" (Psalm 133:1-3). "Again I say to you that if two of you agree on earth concerning anything that they ask, it will be done for them by My Father in heaven. For where two or three are gathered together in My name, I am there in the midst of them" (Matthew 18:19-20).

This law will work for us to cause increase and blessing if we truly believe that there is exponential increase to what we can do if we come into unity of beliefs and purpose with others. The story of the Tower of Babel reveals the depth of this spiritual law. They were walking in such a deep agreement that it is said that "nothing that they propose to do will be withheld from them." This truth is reinforced in Psalm 133 where the Lord says He will "command" His blessing where He finds "brethren dwelling in unity." If we want to do something great for God or if we want to see heaven's resources released abundantly, then it would benefit us greatly to find people of like heart to agree with and be in unity with. It's a great spiritual law.

This law will work against us to restrict and impoverish us if we walk in strife, or if we isolate ourselves and don't connect dynamically with other parts of the body of Christ. Jesus said that a "house divided against itself will not stand" (Matthew 12:25). Division opens the door to defeat. Certainly, we realize that we cannot agree with everyone (or with lies and heresy), but a divisive and chronically untrusting person has a root problem that blocks the ability to have deep agreement with others and thus obstructs the flow of blessing and increase.

This law will bring us into a greater intimacy with God because we will discover that God Himself is in unity with the three parts of His being (Father, Son and Holy Spirit). As we have revelation of how the Godhead interacts with one another, we will be transformed to walk in unity with others.

I delight in this law by joyfully declaring: I walk in great unity and agreement. I am breaking through the obstacles to powerful unity. I am experiencing deep heart and truth connections that bear much fruit.

Law of the Spirit #18
The Law of Tithing
"Try Me in this" (Malachi 3:10)

This law is revealed in the Bible in passages such as: "'Will a man rob God? Yet you have robbed Me! But you say, "In what way have we robbed You?" In tithes and offerings. You are cursed with a curse, for you have robbed Me, *even* this whole nation. Bring all the tithes into the storehouse, that there may be food in My house, And try Me now in this,' says the LORD of hosts, 'If I will not open for you the windows of heaven and pour out for you *such* blessing that *there will not be room* enough *to receive it.* And I will rebuke the devourer for your sakes, So that he will not destroy the fruit of your ground, nor shall the vine fail to bear fruit for you in the field,' says the LORD of hosts; 'And all nations will call you blessed, For you will be a delightful land,' says the LORD of hosts" (Mal. 3:9-12).

This law will work for us to cause increase and blessing if we believe that tithing (giving 10% back to God) is not a fear-motivated command to be obeyed, but rather a timeless spiritual law (principle) that will work for anyone who "tries" it. The above passage in Malachi is a great illustration of how all the laws of the Spirit work. It describes the abundant blessing of sowing to the spirit, but it also emphasizes the curse that results from not doing so. (Remember, curses can only exist when the blessing is absent.) Malachi revealed how God is "robbed" of the opportunity to release blessing because He has little or nothing to work with to do so. This law will work for us mightily if we regularly invest 10% of our increase to God and His kingdom. God says we can do much more with a blessed 90% than an unblessed 100%. (The tithe is a good beginning place of our plan to live a life that taps into the wonders of giving and generosity.)

This law will work against us to restrict and impoverish us if we keep the tithe and spend it on ourselves. Some ask, "Do Christians have to tithe?" My answer to that is another question, "Do Christians have to obey the law of gravity? No, but they get to, and it would be dumb not to." If you study tithing, you will find it was practiced before God's law was revealed to Moses, during the time of the law, and then Jesus reinforced its practice. (See Matthew 23:23.) Although God may lead people differently in the practice of tithing, I believe that if we are called to a local fellowship of believers, then our tithe is best served there (as it reflects the needed commitment to do great things together.)

This law will bring us into a greater intimacy with God because we will discover that God has given us His first and best part (Jesus) because of His love and consistent commitment to us.

I delight in this law by joyfully declaring: Tithing is a main part of my supernatural increase strategy.

Law of the Spirit #19
The Law of Hearing
"Faith comes by hearing" (Romans 10:17)

This law is revealed in the Bible in passages such as: "Then He said to them, 'Take heed what you hear. With the same measure you use, it will be measured to you; and to you who hear, more will be given. For whoever has, to him more will be given; but whoever does not have, even what he has will be taken away from him'" (Mark 4:24-25). "Therefore take heed how you hear. For whoever has, to him *more* will be given; and whoever does not have, even what he seems to have will be taken from him" (Luke 8:18). "So then faith *comes* by hearing, and hearing by the word of God" (Romans 10:17). "Therefore He who supplies the Spirit to you and works miracles among you, *does He do it* by the works of the law, or by the hearing of faith?" (Galatians 3:5). "He who has ears to hear, let him hear" (Matthew 11:15). "You have become dull of hearing" (Hebrews 5:11).

This law will work for us to cause increase and blessing if we listen to and really hear large quantities of Scripture, testimonies, promises, encouragement, prophecies, hope and other expressions of godly truth. Our future abundance is directly linked to our spiritual hearing. "To you who hear, more will be given" (Mark 4:24). This abundance is released in proportion to the amount we hear. "With the same measure you use, it will be measured to you." And we don't just focus on the quantity of our hearing, but also on the quality of our spiritual hearing. (See Luke 8:18.) The wise person realizes it is imperative to cultivate and maintain excitement, wonder, expectation and childlike enthusiasm as we hear the things of God. Our core beliefs are shaped by what we allow ourselves to hear and how we hear it. "Faith comes by hearing" (Romans 10:17). Every plan for forward movement in life needs to include the powerful law of hearing.

This law will work against us to restrict and impoverish us if we are in environments where we hear a great amount of negativity, lies, fear, criticism, worry, anger, selfishness, godlessness, etc. It will also work against us if we hear (believe) lies spoken to us by an authority figure or someone we respect. Finally, we will be restricted in life if we become a person who is dull of hearing and become a "sermon proof" Christian (or testimony proof, hope proof, etc.)

This law will bring us into a greater intimacy with God because we will discover that there is a higher level of hearing in our relationship with God that causes us to come alive in Him. "Man shall not live by bread alone, but by every word that proceeds from the mouth of God" (Matthew 4:4). Prayer is not just our talking to God, but it is also hearing God's "proceeding words" in new ways.

> **I delight in this law by joyfully declaring:** I hear an enormous quantity of good things. I hear in an incredible manner. As a result, I experience great increase.

Law of the Spirit #20
The Law of the Spirit of Life in Christ Jesus
"Christ has redeemed us from the curse of the law" (Galatians 3:13)

This law is revealed in the Bible in passages such as: "For the law of the Spirit of life in Christ Jesus has made me free from the law of sin and death. For what the law could not do in that it was weak through the flesh, God *did* by sending His own Son in the likeness of sinful flesh, on account of sin: He condemned sin in the flesh" (Romans 8:2-3). "Christ has redeemed us from the curse of the law, having become a curse for us (for it is written, *'Cursed is everyone who hangs on a tree'*), that the blessing of Abraham might come upon the Gentiles in Christ Jesus, that we might receive the promise of the Spirit through faith" (Galatians 3:13-14). "I delight in the law of God according to the inward man. But I see another law in my members, warring against the law of my mind, and bringing me into captivity to the law of sin which is in my members. O wretched man that I am! Who will deliver me from this body of death? I thank God – through Jesus Christ our Lord!" (Romans 7:22-25).

This law will work for us to cause increase and blessing if we know that faith in Christ is not only the way to eternal life, but it is also the way to be empowered to follow God's laws. Jesus came to earth because no one could obey the law fully because of our inherited sin nature that came to us through Adam. Jesus created the way for us to become spiritually born again through faith. (See John 3:3.) When this happens, our old sin nature dies and we become a "new creation" with an inner compulsion to follow God's laws. (See 2 Corinthians 5:17, Hebrews 10:16.) This internal drive toward obeying spiritual laws does not make us a Christian, but it is the result of being one. Jesus has made us free from the law of sin and death through the law of the Spirit of life. This freedom comes through embracing a living faith in Jesus (and believing we are dead to sin and alive to obeying God. (See Romans 6:11.)

This law will work against us to restrict and impoverish us if we believe that good works (conduct) is the means to become acceptable to God. Galatians 5:4 reveals that those who have this mentality are actually "cut off" from empowering grace. Unless there is a fresh wave of people being born again, there will be a continuous decline in people's ability to walk in morality and God's laws (because it is impossible to obey God on our own).

This law will bring us into a greater intimacy with God because we will discover that faith and intimacy with Christ is the greatest law that releases power to follow the rest of God's spiritual laws.

I delight in this law by joyfully declaring: The law of the Spirit of life is operating in me mightily and is catalytic for me to follow all other spiritual laws.

Other Laws of the Spirit

The Law of Faith and Believing – "According to your faith let it be to you" (Matthew 10:29). "For assuredly, I say to you, whoever says to this mountain, 'Be removed and be cast into the sea,' and does not doubt in his heart, but believes that those things he says will be done, he will have whatever he says. Therefore I say to you, whatever things you ask when you pray, believe that you receive *them,* and you will have *them* (Mark 11:23-24). "All things are possible to him who believes" (Mark 9:24).

The Law of Love – "Love never fails" (I Corinthians 13:8). "And now abide faith, hope, love, these three; but the greatest of these *is* love" (I Corinthians 13:13). "Perfect love casts out fear" (I John 4:18).

The Law of Seeking God – "He who comes to God must believe that He is, and *that* He is a rewarder of those who diligently seek Him" (Hebrews 11:6). "Seek and you will find" (Matthew 7:7). "I love those who Love Me. And those who seek Me diligently will find Me" (Proverbs 8:17). "And you will seek Me and find Me, when you search for Me with all your heart" (Jeremiah 29:12).

The Law of Courage and Boldness – "'Lord, look on their threats, and grant to Your servants that with all boldness they may speak Your word, by stretching out Your hand to heal, and that signs and wonders may be done through the name of Your holy Servant Jesus.' And when they had prayed, the place where they were assembled together was shaken; and they were all filled with the Holy Spirit, and they spoke the word of God with boldness" (Acts 4:29-31).

The Law of Delighting in the Lord – "Delight yourself also in the LORD, and He shall give you the desires of your heart" (Psalm 37:4).

The Law of Worship and Praise – "Now when they began to sing and to praise, the LORD set ambushes against the people of Ammon, Moab, and Mount Seir, who had come against Judah; and they were defeated" (2 Chronicles 20:22). "But at midnight Paul and Silas were praying and singing hymns to God, and the prisoners were listening to them. Suddenly there was a great earthquake, so that the foundations of the prison were shaken; and immediately all the doors were opened and everyone's chains were loosed" (Acts 16:25-26).

The Law of Prayer – "The effective, fervent prayer of a righteous man avails much" (James 5:16). "Ask, and it will be given to you; seek, and you will find; knock, and it will be opened to you" (Matthew 7:7). "If My people who are called by My name will humble themselves, and pray and seek My face, and turn from their wicked ways, then I will hear from heaven, and will forgive their sin and heal their land" (2 Chronicles 7:14).

About The Author

Steve Backlund is known for his wisdom and practical insights on "how to do life." The students in our ministry school, Bethel School of Supernatural Ministry, love him because he always leaves them encouraged and refreshed in their vision. He has an unusual gift to take the mundane and make it exciting, and to take the familiar and make it new.

Bill Johnson, Bethel Church, Redding, CA
Author of <u>When Heaven Invades Earth</u>

<u>If you enjoy this book go to ignitedhope.com</u>:

- ➤ For sermon downloads of messages by Steve & Wendy
- ➤ To purchase books and resources
- ➤ For information on the Backlund's speaking itinerary
- ➤ To contact Steve or Wendy about speaking to your group
- ➤ For many free helps to inspire your life

Other Books by Steve Backlund

<u>**Igniting Faith in 40 Days**</u> – Written with Wendy, this book is ideal for a 40-day negativity fast and to pour "spiritual gasoline" on your faith and hope.

<u>**Cracks in the Foundation**</u> – This writing examines the negative effects of religious tradition that neutralizes the power of God's promises. Its teachings will repair cracks in your faith foundation so that God can build something great through you.

<u>**Possessing Joy**</u> – The joy of the Lord is our strength, and a merry heart is like good medicine. God has called us to serve Him with gladness. This book will give you incredible keys to do so.

<u>**You're Crazy If You DON'T Talk to Yourself**</u> – LIFE IS IN THE POWER OF THE TONGUE. Jesus did not just THINK His way out of the wilderness and neither can you. Like Jesus we must SPEAK TRUTH to invisible forces and to the mindsets that seek to restrict and defeat us.

<u>**Victorious Mindsets**</u> – What we believe is ultimately more important than what we do. The course of our lives is set by our deepest core beliefs (mindsets). These mindsets are either a stronghold for God's purposes or a playhouse for the enemy of our souls. This book reveals 50 biblical attitudes that are foundational for walking in freedom and power.